Not the Big Sleep

Marie-Louise von Franz, Honorary Patron

**Studies in Jungian Psychology
by Jungian Analysts**

Daryl Sharp, General Editor

NOT THE BIG SLEEP

On having fun, seriously

A Jungian Romance

DARYL SHARP

*For my daughters, Tanya Claire and Jessy Kate,
and for my late friend and snooker partner, Jerry Pethick.*

Library and Archives Canada Cataloguing in Publication

Sharp, Daryl, 1936-
    Not the big sleep: on having fun, seriously: a Jungian
romance / Daryl Sharp.

(Studies in Jungian psychology by Jungian analysts; 112)

Includes bibliographical references and index.

ISBN 1-894574-13-3

1. Self-actualization (Psychology).
2. Jungian psychology.
I. Title. II. Series.

BF175.S492 2005   158.1   C2004-903598-3

INNER CITY BOOKS
Box 1271, Station Q, Toronto, ON M4T 2P4, Canada

Telephone (416) 927-0355 / Fax (416) 924-1814

Web site: www.innercitybooks.net / E-mail: admin@innercitybooks.net

Honorary Patron: Marie-Louise von Franz.
Publisher and General Editor: Daryl Sharp.
Senior Editor: Victoria B. Cowan.

INNER CITY BOOKS was founded in 1980 to promote the
understanding and practical application of the work of C.G. Jung.

Cover: *The Bottle Man* (Le Semeur, Sunlight and Flies), 8 feet tall,
    composed of 386 vari-colored wine bottles; by Canadian sculptor
    Jerry Pethick, Hornby Island, BC, 1985.

Printed and bound in Canada by University of Toronto Press Incorporated

CONTENTS

Preface 7

1   Introduction 9

2   Brillig on the Ball 21

3   A Bedtime Story 30

4   Batting the Ball with Nurse Pam 34

5   On Growing Up 44

6   The Heart as Lonely Hunter 53

7   Love's Labor Lost 60

8   Ballin' with Rachel 68

9   The Razor's Edge 78

10 The Crystal Ball 90

11 Momma Mia 102

12 Ballin' the Jack 112

Bibliography 121

Index 123

See final page for other books by Daryl Sharp

There is a fine old story about a student who came to a rabbi and said, "In the olden days there were men who saw the face of God. Why don't they any more?" The rabbi replied, "Because nowadays no one can stoop so low."

One must stoop a little in order to fetch water from the stream.

—C.G. Jung, *Memories, Dreams, Reflections.*

romance, noun & adjective, & verb intransitive:
1. Prose or (rarely) verse tale with scenes and incidents remote from everyday life; class of literature consisting of such tales; set of facts, episode, love affair, etc., suggesting such tales by its strangeness or moving nature; atmosphere characterizing such tales, sympathetic imaginativeness.
2. exaggeration, picturesque falsehood.
3. short piece of simple character.
4. to exaggerate or distort the truth, draw the long-bow.

—*Concise Oxford Dictionary.*

There are things in the psyche which I do not produce, but which produce themselves and have their own life.

—C.G. Jung, *Memories, Dreams, Reflections.*

Preface

This book began life some years ago with the title *Balls: A Jungian Approach to the Meaning of Balls and Ball Games in Dreams*. Such a book did not exist, and I thought I was well equipped to write it.

I began by establishing the bare bones of balls:

Physically and visually, a ball is easily identified by its spherical shape. It is distinguished by having three dimensions, whereas circles, rectangles, triangles, pentagons and the like must make do with two. Also, in the world of three-dimensional objects—boxes, spires, obelisks, ovoids, pyramids, etc.—balls are undoubtedly the aristocrats, having the greatest internal volume for a given surface area.

Balls come in all sizes and compositions. They are found in nature and are manufactured according to their intended use in various sports or other pastimes. Balls are containers. Some are hollow, full of air. Others are solid, filled with all kinds of unknown "stuff"—arcane ingredients known only to their trade-marked purveyors.

Symbolically, balls are much, much more than their obvious shape or what, if anything, is in them. I have become aware of just how much more due to the many dreams involving balls and ball games I have been privy to in my practice over the past twenty-five years. And some of them were my own.

Among ball games, my own long-standing passion is snooker, derived from billiards which is father to the more popular game of pool. In my younger years I also played tennis, squash, volleyball, basketball and baseball. In those days I was unconscious. I had in mind only the goal—winning—and no idea of what balls and the playing of such games, far less dreaming about them, might mean psychologically.

*

Well, that was a good start, or so I thought. Over the next few months I pored over hundreds of dreams of balls and ball games, looking for a common thread. I didn't find one, except for the fact that they were all absolutely incomprehensible without some knowledge of the context—the dreamer's life. But I got fired up all the same and prepared an outline. I plodded along, as single-minded and goal-oriented as ever.

I did not reckon with the unconscious.

It turned out that where I had a will, there was no way. Pure and simple, I got sidetracked. Perhaps I was unwittingly seeking transcendence, a spiritual uplift to compensate my generally mundane way of being. I don't know about that, but clearly there was something other than balls in store for me, which is what this book is about. Perhaps I had become somber beyond my years (senex) and it was imperative that I become young again (puer), at least to some extent.

*

Turn back the clock some forty years.

As a struggling young writer whose walls were papered with rejection slips, I came to feel that life was the shits. Immersed in my narcissistic bubble, I conceived of writing a book called *The World Is a Turd*. In that book I would take my revenge on all those who over the years had crossed me or thwarted my desires, from elementary school through high school, university and beyond. I would tell all: the nitty-gritty details, from the bully in Grade One who took all my marbles, to the loss of my teenage sweetheart to Paul Anka, on then in college to my best friend seducing my virginal girlfriend before I did, and finally to what happened to end my marriage. I would immolate the lot of them. I could get high just thinking of it. And one way or another I regularly did—dope, booze, sex.

What a friggin' mess.

That book idea went nowhere, and just as well. The reality was that I was in an outhouse of my own making. I had crapped out. The world was not a turd; I was. How simple that now sounds. But it took several years of analysis for me to wake up to the existence of my shadow, to realize that my attitude, my way of being in the world, was the real problem. So I then resolved to write a book entitled *I Thought the World Was a Turd Until I Stooped and Scooped.*

All in all, this book is simply my latest foray into the unknown.

Oh, and I changed the title, again.

1
Introduction

I did not actually call Adam Brillig out of retirement; rather I felt his presence, his coming, if you get my drift. Perhaps you have experienced the aura that surrounds a certain time of day, a certain situation or person. Adam has that and it precedes him, perhaps to prepare those who one way or another are bound to be affected. Well, let's just say that Brillig has charisma. Of course he's no Sean Connery or Alec Guiness, but he has a goodly measure of "it."

Adam and I had collaborated in the writing of several books,[1] but that was a few years ago and I had not been in touch with him since. So much to do! So little time! Nevertheless, when I became interested in the subject of balls, he was the first help-mate to come to mind and so I sought him out.

I found Adam flat on his back in bed, on the ground floor of a private nursing home in downtown Toronto.[2] He had a spacious room with a patio and a garden. A bright yellow wheelchair by the bed was state of the art—hydraulics, electronics, pneumatic brakes, automatic drive, cruise control, short-wave radio, eight-inch TV, global positioning system (GPS), cell-phone and more. It moved up and down, sideways, back and forth, all at the touch of a big red mouse-ball. Physically handicapped persons have navigated the globe in less.

---

[1] See my **Brillig Trilogy**: 1) *Chicken Little: The Inside Story;* 2) *Who Am I, Really: Personality, Soul and Individuation;* and 3) *Living Jung: The Good and the Better.* Adam and I pioneered the "Jungian romance" genre of writing, and to my knowledge are still its only practitioners.

[2] In case readers are wondering how I found Adam so easily, it was because I was paying the shot; well, from his share of royalties. He did not know this. Adam thought his upkeep was provided by an old girlfriend—Camilla, I think her name was—who lived in Nassau with two toy poodles and an oil magnate. I happily maintained this fiction because Adam is very fond of women, especially old girlfriends who still like him. I also felt a sense of responsibility, as I was his closest living relative, being the son of his first wife's brother's third cousin (my father).

Adam's persona was impeccable. He was dressed to the nines as usual, even in bed: Armani shirt and Laura Ashley cravat, black Hugo Boss trousers, socks by Tommy. I bet his cherished Bally boots were in the closet, just in case. His few head hairs had been trimmed by Cathy of the David Austin salon on Mount Pleasant. (I knew this because she was my hairdresser too.) He was clean shaven and gave off a faint whiff of Old Spice, just like my dear old dad, rest his soul.

Adam was never much taller than a dwarf—gnomish comes to mind—but even so he had shrunk further, as old folks often do. His color was good though, and all in all he seemed fit.

"Looks like you're doing okay, you devil," I smiled.

"Spare me your sweet talk," grumped Adam, putting down Jung's *Modern Man in Search of a Soul*. "I have resources you can't even imagine. You're ungrateful and uncaring."

"Pardon me?" I was taken aback.

"Where have you been?" he complained. "You don't know your balls from your ears. I've been chewing my nails, eating my heart out for company. You'd be nothing without me, nothing! And you abandoned me!"

He ranted on but it didn't bother me. Adam was eighty-eight years old, though he could easily pass for eighty-six.[3] He has a curmudgeon side, but he's not intransigent and his heart is open for more than bypass surgery. I know him almost as well as I know myself. He's always been more than willing to change, which as a matter of fact I'm usually not. As well, Adam has a vast store of knowledge, and his experience, analytically and otherwise, exceeds mine by plenty. I would hate to lose him.

"Hey! You didn't exactly fall all over yourself trying to contact me, did you?"

"That is true," he nodded. "But I'm older! And I'm also an invalid. I would appreciate some respect."

---

[3] Adam received his Diploma in Analytical Psychology from the C.G. Jung Institute in Zurich in 1956. I graduated from the same place in 1978. So you see he had a good 20+ years on me—more or less the difference in our ages.

He pronounced invalid in-*valid.* I didn't like that. It implied a degree of self-pity that was out of character.

The ECG monitor burped. A nurse appeared in about two seconds: attractive, middle-aged, flaming red hair and long eyelashes. She adjusted a few dials, patted Adam's head and chucked his chin.

"Professor Brillig, everything okay? Can I get you some lemonade, water, cuppa tea, anything?"

Adam smiled at her and glowed. "A tumbler of the hard stuff wouldn't go amiss, but I'm just fine with you here."

I liked that. Always the ladies' man, an incorrigible flirt, the old coot still had some juice. The first time we worked together he seduced my Rachel, the rascal.[4]

"This is Nurse Pam," he said. "Pam, meet young Razor, he thinks he's a writer."

"I am definitely on the cutting edge," I grinned, "a bleeding heart. Pleased to meetcha."

"Charmed, I'm sure," she smiled. Good teeth. "Call if you need me." And she trotted off. Good legs too.

Then I got down to business. "Now Adam, hear me out."

I then proceeded to outline what I had in mind for my book on balls, chapter by chapter:

1. A Brief Overview of the Field of Play
   - etymology
   - balls in mythology
   - ball games as mirrors of life
2. Major Ball Games
   - Baseball
   - Soccer
   - Volleyball
   - Pool/Snooker/Billiards
   - Basketball
   - Tennis

---

[4] See *Chicken Little,* pp. 89f.

- Squash
- Golf
- Ping Pong

3. Balls in Nature
    - planets, sun and moon
    - testicles
    - eyeball
    - hairball
    - fireball
    - kidney stones
    - gallstones
    - lightning balls
    - hail [ice pellets]
    - oranges, apples, kumquats, etc.
    - fish eggs [caviar]
    - ball of dough?
    - raindrops
    - ovaries?
    - snowballs!

4. Miscellaneous Balls & Ball Games
    - boules/bocce/petanque
    - 5- and 10-pin bowling
    - beach ball
    - lawn bowling
    - softball
    - marbles
    - croquet
    - cricket
    - lacrosse [Canada's national sport]
    - pinball
    - medicine ball
    - roulette
    - bombs
    - fairground balls [penny a pitch]

- cannonball
- gumball
- mothballs
- bee-bees
- ball bearings

5. Ball Wannabes
    - American football
    - rugby
    - hockey puck
    - curling stone
    - shuttlecock
    - eggs
    - mandalas
    - gyroscope
    - buttons
    - traffic lights?
    - donuts?
    - ball-point pens?
    - bubbles!

6. Music of the Spheres
    - astrology
    - crystal balls [fortune telling]
    - flying saucers?
    - God-balls?

7. Balls in Song & Dance
    - ballrooms
    - ballin' the jack [dance; also "to risk everything"]

8. Balls in Fairy Tales
    - The Crystal Ball [Grimm]
    - ball of thread leading to the treasure
    - golden ball [child motif]

9. Idiomatic Balls
    - balls to you!
    - have someone's balls for breakfast

- he/she has no balls
- break/bust someone's balls
- ballsy lady/man
- to eyeball someone
- [the] ball's in your court/corner/park
- get the ball rolling
- to ball a woman [have sex]
- play ball [co-operate]
- the whole ball of wax
- to have a ball [good time]
- behind the eight ball
- keep your eye on the ball [pay attention]
- that's the way the ball bounces
- belle of the ball
- ball and chain [marriage, etc.]
- to blackball someone
- screwball/cornball
- play hardball [in business]
- in the ball-park [close estimate]

10. Questionable Balls
    - Rice Krispies, Cheerios, etc.
    - pipe bowls
    - ice cube balls [in refrigerator]
    - buoys!

Adam rolled his eyes.

"Okay, okay, so it's not exhaustive," I said with mock modesty, for in fact I thought it was definitive, that nothing had been left out, "but it's a start."

Adam said: "It exhausts me just to hear it. Anyway, you missed Chinese checkers, jaw-breakers, balloons and those numbered bingo balls that tumble in a cage."

My heart fell. I'd rather be appreciated for what I do instead of criticized for what I don't. But I rallied my forces.

"Listen Adam, chapters on particular games would explain how they're played—rules and regulations, etc.—then go on with clinical examples of their occurrence in dreams and how these might be interpreted according to Jung's theories of compensation and the self-regulation of the psyche.[5] And for the rest we could wing it. Jeez! I could probably get a grant to do the research! What do you think?"

Adam pondered.

Adam's eyes glaze over when he ponders. His lips quiver, he sniffs and snuffles, burps, picks his nose, pulls his right earlobe (remember Bogart doing that in *The Big Sleep?),* moves his jaw up and down like a raptor, and makes other moves and gestures too salty to mention here. I am careful not to interrupt Adam when he is pondering. This isn't out of respect—though I'm not lacking in that for him—no, it's because when he's pondered enough he might say something I can use in a book.

Nurse Pam came in and plumped his pillows, fine-tuned the IV. She lit a couple of candles to dispel the gloom. That said something—a romantic? Environmentalist? You just never know these days. She pecked Adam's forehead and massaged his neck and shoulders. Behind his back she winked at me and flashed a Colgate smile.

Kerbloom! I was hooked. I Morse-coded her with my eyes, inviting her for dinner. She nodded and blinked back: Wednesday's good, thanks.

After a few minutes Adam coughed.

"It is a weighty subject, well worth our attention."

"What subject is that?" I asked, my brains suddenly quite addled.

"Balls, laddie, balls!"

Boy, was I glad to hear that.

---

[5] Compensation is a process whereby psychic balance is established or maintained. For instance, if the conscious attitude is too one-sided, the dream takes the opposite tack; if the conscious attitude is more or less appropriate, the dream seems satisfied with pointing out minor variations; and if the conscious attitude is entirely adequate, then the dream may even support it.

As for self-regulation, Jungian theory holds that the individual psyche knows both its limits and its potential. If the former are being exceeded, or the latter not realized, a breakdown occurs; i.e., the psyche itself acts to correct the situation.

Then he frowned.

"But your linear thinking makes me want to throw up. Dear boy, there are other ways. For a start, we mustn't slip into the o-void, for that would take us too far afield.[6] As well, we'd have to set boundaries, be selective, else we'd be overwhelmed by the sheer weight of information."

"Indeed! Tell me," I said, for after all I was there to listen.

We talked all afternoon; argued, agreed; argued again, agreed; argued some more; agreed to disagree.

About three o'clock Nurse Pam brought us a tasty snack: goose liver paté, smoked salmon, crackers and sesame buns, Danish havarti, Swedish caviar. Oh, and a chilled bottle of chardonnay from the Ontario Niagara peninsula. I could have stayed all night. Adam was in good form. I was laughing and crying at the same time, high on him.

Pam came back about five.

"Professor Brillig, time for your bath," she said.

"Blast!" grumped Adam. "Just when I get going! This is the most fun I've had in years. You're a spoil-sport!"

Pam purred in his ear.

"Right, okay, if I must," sighed Adam.

I was on my way out when he raised his head. "Laddie, don't forget the ball dream that took you into analysis."

As if I could.

On the way out I tucked my outline away. A chilly thrill ran up my spine. Brillig was out of the closet! On life support, perhaps, but still brilligant. I reflected that the thing I most liked about Adam—over and above his mental acumen, his twinkly eyes and trickster nature—was that he takes me back to Jung. I looked forward to that.

And to Nurse Pam, of course.

---

[6] The experience of being lost in the void—a sense of emptiness characteristic of the midlife blues—is not unusual, preceding the coming to consciousness of the Self, regulating center of the psyche. Or perhaps Adam used the term to refer to the deep abyss of unconsciousness which many religions consider to be the condition of nothingness that existed before the gods or humans came into being. He may have added the prefix "o-" to fit the context.

Back home in my modest Victorian mansion in the heart of the city, I summoned my factotum.

"Luigi, escargots tonight, in their shells, with that garlic butter you make so well. Then steak tartar with Dijon mustard, a small salad of mixed greens doused with Paul Newman's balsamic vinaigrette, and half a liter of Dingbat '96.[7] I'd like an apricot parfait for afters."

"Very good, sir. Would you like your Dingbat with an ice-cube? You usually do."

"Yes, please! And thanks for reminding me."

Truth be told, I felt a bit woozy from the time with Adam. I was excited with the new project; my mind raced with possibilities. Inflated? Indeed I was—that's bound to happen when the conscious mind is suddenly privy to what's been languishing unnoticed in the unconscious. It happens to writers all the time. You get a rush of insight where all is clear; you know everything, the big picture. And for the next few years you grapple with how to express it in a single paragraph or sentence, or one word even. And you finally give up and write a book about how it's actually impossible to do any of that.

Well, maybe that's what I'm doing here. And is that so bad? I mean I have to do something or go bonkers doing nothing. Maybe I will mirror myself in what I write, discover a new way to be.

In terms of Jung's model of typology, I'm mostly a sensation type—a down-to-earth, sure-footed, no-nonsense type of guy. I am at my best doing what's right in front of me. Well, think about it: if I don't, who will? However, this way of orienting oneself in the world has its drawbacks. For instance, I feel insecure on shaky ground and so I steer well clear of the unpredictable, which does not faze my opposite number—the intuitive, a.k.a. my shadow—who can barely fry an egg or boil water, let alone remember where he left his keys, but is right at home with the unknown and thrives on possibilities.

So, it seemed a safe bet that my inferior intuition was now in full

---

[7] Not to be confused with the computer typeface called Zapf Dingbats. Dingbat wine is a fruity pinot made from virgin grapes grown in the Ardenne region of France. It is more akin to a Clos de Vougeot burgundy than to anything found on computers.

flight. Was this really me? I pulled my book on types off the shelf and read what I'd written some fifteen years ago:

> Although accurate in recording physical reality, the sensation function tends to be sluggish, slow-moving. . . . This type easily gets stuck in a rut, bogged down in the routine of the present moment. Attuned to the here and now, what is, they have the greatest difficulty imagining what might be, the possibilities that are the natural domain of the intuitive.[8]

That's a fair description of me—sluggish and slow-moving, and ruts are my second home—but on the other hand, when anima and shadow get into the act, all bets are off, for they are the keepers of my dormant intuition, and if they conspire to let it out—in accordance with their role in regulating my psychic health—I am obliged to tag along.

I read more:

> Intuition is constantly on the lookout for new opportunities, new fields to conquer. Existing situations are not interesting for long; the intuitive is quickly bored by "things as they are." Intuition can ferret out possibilities, but to actualize them requires the focusing abilities of sensation and thinking.[9]

Well said! I have those focusing abilities in abundance, to a fault even. And I am seldom bored by "things as they are," which as a matter of fact I depend on for my sanity. But without something to focus on—which is to say, possibilities—I am little more than a drudge.

I reflected too on my off-hand thought:

"And to Nurse Pam, of course."

I had gone to see Adam with a book on my mind, and then I was smitten by the sparkling eyes of his nurse. I mean, talk about projection. This is anima for sure, I thought. Now, I'm no stranger to bewitchment, and I know my inner woman pretty well, but that never stopped me—or anyone I know—from being caught up in a web of illusion, or *maya*, as they call it in the East: The Big Spider.

Well, so what? That's no reason not to explore the feeling. You

---

[8] *Personality Types: Jung's Model of Typology,* p. 83.
[9] Ibid., p. 61.

only have to be concerned about projection when the other person doesn't meet your expectations, which often as not are unconscious. I don't know, Nurse Pam might even have something of interest to say about balls. Stranger things have happened. I resolved to go with the flow. That's not usually my best crack at bat, but I'd give it a go.

All in all, I had in mind what Jung called the process of individuation—becoming the person you were meant to be, conscious of your strengths and weaknesses—part and parcel of which is how what happens in your life affects your head and your heart, sometimes in spite of either. In fact, Jung thought that achieving the fullest development of one's personality was a never-completed, lifelong task—a journey on which one sets out hopefully toward a dimly perceived destination that one never reaches. . . .

Indeed, individuation can be a lonely road, with plenty of metaphorical potholes and sometimes actual ones too. When I was at a low point last year I literally drove my Volkswagen into a depression in the road. Its bottom was scraped so badly that I had to replace the whole friggin' engine, and then my insurance went up because it was classified as a "single vehicle accident"! . . .

We can plan ahead all we want and think we're safe, well contained, all the bases covered, but then we can still be balled over—pardon me, bowled—by the unexpected. What can you do? Expect the unexpected, that's what. The world turns, with us on it. We can thank our lucky stars if we don't fall off.

Life itself is like a ball; it rolls along, taking us with it. Basically, we're just along for the ride and we might as well enjoy it as complain about the bumps.

Well, that's the way I often feel after a tasty meal and a few glasses of Dingbat. I loosen up. I toy with ideas, move into a mental space where just about anything can happen. I have fun being me and a few others as well.

I thought too of the relationship between erotic feelings and being creative. For me they've always gone hand in hand. What is that all about? Are there others who feel the same? Does it have anything to do with typology? Balls? Ball games?

Maybe I'd get into that later. So much to do! So little time! For the moment I was content just to be alive.

"Perfect parfait, Luigi," I said, licking my lips. "Prepare my bath if you will, there's a good fellow. And use those salts I picked up in Baden-Baden. Oh, and a touch of bubbles too, what the hell."

"Very good, sir, very very good."

I put on a Sinatra CD and fell into a reverie.

Fly me to the moon,
Let me play among the stars,
Let me see what spring is like on Jupiter and Mars,
In other words, hold my hand,
In other words, please be true,
In other words, I love you.[10]

Henri Matisse, *Les Joueurs de Boules* (The Boules Players), 1908.
(Hermitage Museum, Saint Petersburg, Russia)

---

[10] Lyrics by Bart Howard.

2
Brillig on the Ball

A few days later I was back with Adam. I had made some notes, but I still had no sure direction. I wanted to hear what he'd come up with in the meantime.

Adam was in bed reading a 1952 issue of *Amazing Stories* edited by Arthur C. Clarke. I had to smile, it brought back so many memories. As a teenager in a backwater town in Nova Scotia I was obsessed with science-fiction. Every Friday after school I raced my buddy Bomba to the corner store to be the first to eyeball the latest *Amazing Stories* or *Galaxy* or whatever new mag Hugo Gernsbach had started. When I got to university I gave science-fiction up for women, but that's another story.

"I like reliving the old times," said Adam, "the thrill of being young, on the brink of life. The sheer magic of it all! I've faltered and fallen, but I can honestly say I've never fettered my imagination."

"You can say that again," I nodded.

"I've faltered and fallen, but I've never fettered my imagination," obliged Adam.

I had brought a bouquet of flowers—daisies, crocuses, hyacinth, daffodils. I found a vase on the windowsill and filled it with water.

"Can I get you anything?" I asked.

"A Kleenex, thanks."

Adam thoroughly blew his nose.

"I've given your project considerable thought," he said at last. "What is behind the ubiquitous interest in ball games? What is behind dreams of *playing* ball games? These phenomena are so universal that there must be an archetype involved. But just what is it?"

"Balls are obviously symbols of wholeness," I said, "and ball games, well, I see them as metaphors for the process of individuation. Balls connote the personality in three dimensions, as opposed to mandalas, which of course are flat, or at least the traditional ones we know are.

21

As a matter of fact, I like to think of balls as exploded mandalas."

Exploded mandalas! Cripes! That was an absolutely new and un-considered thought, but I wasn't displeased with it. Sometimes things come out of left field and you just have to accept them as gifts from the gods. Listen to this, for example:

> Newton's notion that gravity was a universal which acted at enormous dis-tances was a leap of the imagination which must have seemed absurd until he was able to demonstrate it mathematically. Kekulé's discovery of the ring structure of organic molecules originated from a dream-like vision of atoms combining in chains which then formed into coils like snakes eat-ing their own tails [e.g., the uroborus]. Einstein's special theory of relativ-ity depended on his being able to imagine how the universe might appear to an observer travelling at near the speed of light.[11]

Adam tapped his fingers on his forehead. He does this when he's thinking deep thoughts, or so I imagine. You can never tell with Adam; just when you think he's fallen asleep, he comes to life.

"I am recalling," he said, "that ever since Plato's *Timaeus,* tradi-tional philosophical thinking—not its modern hybrid, which to my mind is more like a kind of convoluted logic or semantics than phi-losophy as I have known it—has held that the soul is a sphere. Per-sonally I see no reason to dispute that."

"Perhaps it has something to do with instinct," I replied. "As you know, Jung used the simile of the spectrum to illustrate the difference between instinct and archetype. Do you recall this passage?" I read from my notes:

> The dynamism of instinct is lodged as it were in the infra-red part of the spectrum, whereas the instinctual image lies in the ultra-violet part. . . . The realization and assimilation of instinct never take place at the red end, i.e., by absorption into the instinctual sphere, but only through integra-tion of the image which signifies and at the same time evokes the in-stinct.[12]

---

[11] Anthony Storr, *Solitude*, p. 67.

[12] "On the Nature of the Psyche," *The Structure and Dynamics of the Psyche,* CW 8, par. 414. (CW refers throughout to *The Collected Works of C.G. Jung)*

"And consider this," I went on, handing him my rough sketch. "It shows the relationship between instinct and archetype as Jung saw it."

INSTINCTS	ARCHETYPES
infrared ———————————————————— ultraviolet	
(**Physiological:** body symptoms, instinctual perceptions, etc.)	(**Psychological:** spirit, dreams, conceptions, images, fantasies, etc.)

"Laddie," said Adam irritably. "I'm not daft. I know that Jung saw an archetype as a primordial, structural element of the human psyche—a universal tendency to form certain ideas and images and to behave in certain ways. Instincts are the physiological counterparts of archetypes. And complexes—well, you know, all those painful buttons that give us a hard time when they're pushed—arise from our individual experience in the here and now, putting skin and flesh on the collective bones of instinct and archetype."

"Thank you!" I said, wishing I'd thought of putting it that way.

Adam reached under his bed and pulled out a case-bound volume of Jung's Collected Works, in fact the same one I'd just quoted from. He thumbed through some dog-eared yellow post-its and stopped.

"Listen to what Jung says":

The question of where instincts come from and how they were acquired is extraordinarily complicated. The fact that they are invariably inherited does nothing to explain their origin . . . . In certain cases it is impossible to conceive how any learning and practice could ever have come about. Let us take as an example the incredibly refined instinct of propagation in the yucca moth *(Pronuba yuccasella).* The flowers of the yucca plant open for one night only. The moth takes the pollen from one of the flowers and kneads it into a little pellet. Then it visits a second flower, cuts open the pistil, lays its eggs between the ovules and then stuffs the pellet into the funnel-shaped opening of the pistil. Only once in its life does the moth carry out this complicated operation.[13]

---

[13] "Instinct and the Unconscious," ibid., par. 268.

"There!" said Adam. "It's plain as can be."

I took the book and read the passage for myself. It made little sense to me. I passed it back to him.

"It's interesting enough," I lied, "but so what? I'm afraid you lost me. What do pollen, eggs, pistils and ovules have to do with balls or ball games?"

Adam took his own good time. Nurse Pam bounced in and took his temperature. I took her measure. We eyed each other and smiled. We'd had a ball on Wednesday. We hadn't played a whole game, but we had talked about the ground rules.

"Don't you get it?" said Adam. "The yucca moth takes the pollen and kneads it into a pellet—a little round ball, you see—and runs with it. It achieves its destiny by doing what it was meant to do. It individuates! Its behavior is a metaphor for a hole in one in golf, a home run in baseball, a perfect drop-shot in squash, and on and on. Never mind that 'once in its life' bit; the yucca moth is not conscious. We humans are privileged to be that; well, some of us, some of the time. So we can do it over and over!"

"Adam, you are babbling," I said. "Just what is this 'it' you think we can do?"

He got so excited he nearly fell out of bed.

"Dumbo! We can do the improbable, and more than once! We can pistulate ovules till the cows come home!"

I shook my head. That was way over the top, even for Adam. I left him to his ravings and sought out Nurse Pam. I found her at work in the kitchen making ham and egg quiches for lunch. I crept up from behind and wrapped my arms around her. I barely resisted licking her neck.

"Get off my back," she laughed, "I'm busy."

Pam's voice had a tinkle to it that reminded me of the Hungarian tradesman who comes down my street every month or so, trailing a large circular carborundum stone on wheels and ringing a bell.

Tinkle! Tinkle! "Hear ye, hear ye! I sharpen knives!"

Tinkle! Tinkle!

With a little stretch of the imagination, he was a god of sorts, sent down from Olympus to sharpen our wits.[14] And with a ball-wannabe Philosophers' Stone as well.

Pam and I made a tentative date for dinner and a movie and I went back to Adam. It is true that I have an active fantasy life, but I also like to be productive. Adam was watching a program on the mating habits of South American three-toed sloths. The sound was off.

"Take me outside," he said. "Unhook me."

I did the necessary, helped him into his Ferrari and wheeled him onto the patio. It was hot and humid, as it often is in Toronto mid-July, but a breeze off the lake made it bearable. We were sun-dappled under Japanese maples and lindens, surrounded by rhododendrons, euonymous and climbing hydrangeas.

"I had another thought," said Adam. "What about balls as transitional objects—breast substitutes?"

I nodded. It was an interesting idea. I did not know a lot about the object relations school of psychology, but I did recall reading about so-called transitional objects—blankets, dolls, teddy-bears and the like—as representing intermediate stages between a child's attachment to the mother and its later attachment to other "objects," including people the child comes to love and depend on.[15]

"Well, if so," I said, "would it mean that an adult interested in ball games was still a kid at heart? Do you think one has to become disinterested in ball games in order to be a grown-up?"

Adam shrugged. "How would I know?"

Okay, so his curmudgeon complex had a hold of him. I could roll with that.

---

[14] As a sharp cutting tool, a knife represents the faculty of discrimination, which as a matter of fact is involved in the writing of books as well as the practice of psychology. "The knife, . . . with its powers of penetration and separation is a potent masculine emblem. . . . Dividing into parts, separating this from that, is the process by which consciousness develops. The alchemists described this process as *separatio.* Jung calls it differentiation." (Eve Jackson, *Food and Transformation: Imagery and Symbolism of Eating,* pp. 55f.)

[15] See D.W. Winnicott, "Transitional Objects and Transitional Phenomena," in *Through Paediatrics to Psycho-Analysis,* pp. 229ff.

"I don't think that being a kid at heart is all that bad," I said, "as long as you know the difference between being a kid and being a grown-up, when to be one and not the other . . . that's crucial, don't you think?"

Adam did not respond. I contemplated the flora.

He spoke up at last.

"Talk about ball games," he wheezed. "I was never good at basketball, baseball or squash, but I did play a lot of snooker in my time."

"You did?!"

This was a complete surprise to me. I knew something of his mountain-climbing exploits and sea-faring adventures, and rather more of his youthful interest in modern European literature and philosophy—Kafka, Rilke, Sartre, Kierkegaard, Nietzsche, Camus, etc., all those heady existentialists who inflamed me too until I got fed up with angst and sought food for the heart—but Adam playing snooker? It just didn't fit.

"You playing snooker?" I said aloud. "I don't know why, but it just doesn't fit."

"What you don't know about me," sniffed Adam, "not to mention the myriad other things in the world that have escaped your attention, would fill a soccer field. Did you know that three golden balls were in the coat of arms of the Lombard family of the Medici, who in the fifteenth century were the greatest money-lenders of their day, hence the sign over a pawnbroker's shop?"

I might have known that at some time, but I don't retain arcane knowledge for long. I just looked at him.

"Huh," said Adam," I thought not. Or that in ancient Rome generals and sons of knights wore a golden ball as a charm to protect them from the evil eye?"

I shook my head.

"Never mind," said Adam cheerfully. He does love to get the upper hand, and it was no skin off my nose to give it to him.

And then, out of his inside breast pocket, Adam pulled a single sheet of paper, creased and yellowed, which he proceeded to unfold and hand to me.

"What do you think of this?"

Here is what I read:

I took the Aussie Guru handily in the first round. He was edgy and runnin' scared. He could hardly make a shot and his cue ball kept ending up in a pocket. He maintained a semblance of composure but you could tell the chagrin was building on account of the way he ground his teeth & cursed at his cue. I finished with the highest score recorded at Central Billiards since Brillig vs. Westby, April '97. I got a star for that, worth ten bucks cash on the line.

I broke the balls for the second round feeling very confident, perhaps a wee bit light-headed if the truth be known, but loaded for bear. Aussie's first shot—a wing-bank off the balk cushion into the side—brought me down somewhat. His next shot fouled and left the cue ball in position for me to easily pot 2 blacks and a pink. Then I sewered, dirty commie bastard! After that Aussie proceeded to shoot the pants off me. I couldn't make a thing, or when I did I scratched. He couldn't miss. His end-game was faultless, snookering me time and time again. He finished with the highest score since Brillig vs. Pethick, June '93—and a star.

I chalked up especially carefully for the third round tie-breaker. Aussie stood there with his *sang-froid* hanging out. I can take him, I thought. After all, I had a walk around the cemetery this morning at 8 a.m. I'm fit and he's still reeling from the champagne at the birthday party last night. He's had a lucky run, that's all. Happens all the time, then bam! back on the mat. But I was mistook. Still swaggering from the inflation of the first round, I was dealt a heavy blow by the gods: I sewered off the break! Dirty commie bastard!

We then played evenly, Aussie making an impossible 3-cushion bank to the top left; me holding my own with a sweet bank cross-side. We went down to the wire, just pink (6 pts.) and black (7 pts.) left, me up 6 points, my shot. Pink was game ball if I made it. I thought of a lovely lady's smile and miscued! Guru golfed the pink into the corner and brought his cue ball in line with the black into the side. That was it. Another star for him, another tenner from me.

I chuckled. Snooker may seem to be a benign, stressless pastime, but I knew it to be a cut-throat business occasioning high anxiety in the best of players.

"Was that a real game?" I asked.

Adam grinned. "Well, I did tweak it a bit. When balls collide I see sparks and hear music."

I nodded. "The music of the spheres."

Celestial harmony, the cosmic chorus. Pythagoras was into that, and according to Jung so was Goethe.[16] It is said that hearing the music of the spheres means you're on the right track. I've heard it myself when I was in love. That's almost all I know about the music of the spheres.

"I see some sparks between you and Pam," said Adam. "It's as if Hephaestus, Greek god of the anvil, was banging up a storm. Is there music too?"

"We sparkle plenty. We banter, we laugh. And we giggle a lot."

"Banter is good," nodded Adam. "Sparks are better. Jung saw sparks as wisps of divine light, a sign that the soul has been activated.[17] And giggling is a dead giveaway. But of course Pam is married."

Well, it was a good bet that anyone worth knowing at my age would already be attached, one way or another. I wouldn't lose heart for that. Winning fair lady is a heroic task. So you meet a dragon along the way. He is no hero who runs home to mother. And mine was no longer around, rest her soul, so I was obliged to go it alone anyway.

"Yes," I said, "but maybe not forever. Without sparks, what is there? The big sleep. I think many couples stay together due to inertia. Just as a ball stays at rest until it is made to move by an outside force, and then continues to roll until some other force stops or redirects it, so relationships can go nowhere, just rolling along . . . and then sometimes, out of the blue, an outside force—let's call it a spark, why not—rolls one of the partners toward someone else. I call this the Rolling Ball Theory."

I hadn't fully developed this theory but I was working on it. So much to do, so little time!

---

[16] See *Symbols of Tranformation,* CW 5, pars. 235ff.

[17] See "On the Nature of the Psyche," *The Structure and Dynamics of the Psyche,* CW 8, par. 430.

"Balls will be balls," said Adam, "but that's not the whole story. In a human being it might instead be an *inside* force, an irresistible desire, an undeniable need even, for change. All in the service of one's individuation, of course."

"That is true," I agreed. "No one person can fill all our needs all the time. We can plumb our own depths to some extent, but we still need others to mirror who we are."

Adam said: "Maybe that's why Jung believed that the prerequisite for a good marriage is the license to be unfaithful."

"You made that up!" I cried.

"Did not. You'll find it in *The Freud/Jung Letters.*"[18]

I said nothing, but I was thinking: Did Jung toss that off the top of his head in a candid moment? Did he really believe it, or was it merely a self-serving remark to rationalize his long-standing affair with Toni Wolff?[19] As I was not in the habit of gainsaying Jung, I let it pass.

Anyway, I have always been more interested in what Jung thought and said and wrote, than in how he behaved in his private life. So he had feet of clay, don't we all. Let those without sin throw the first boule, and I'll throw it right back.

"Alas," sighed Adam, "extramarital affairs lead to break-ups more often than to kiss-and-make-ups."

Yes, Adam had had his share of those, and so had I.

---

[18] Indeed. See William McGuire, ed., *The Freud/Jung Letters,* p. 289.

[19] An account of their relationship from a feeling point of view—including how and why Jung's wife Emma accepted it—is presented in Barbara Hannah's book, *Jung: His Life and Work (A Biographical Memoir),* which overall, in my opinion, is still one of the best biographies of Jung. My other pick, for thinking types, would be Marie-Louise von Franz's *C.G. Jung: His Myth in Our Time.*

3
A Bedtime Story

In bed that night I felt grateful for Pam's presence, though *in absentia*. She lived in my head, but she also had a life of her own. I knew she liked crossword puzzles, chilled white wine and card games. She didn't like to cook. She did like to jog and swim. She didn't play golf, tennis, squash, Scrabble or backgammon, but she said she was not too bad at cribbage and poker, and played a mean hand of bridge. Her husband made his mark coaching a college football team and was now a big-wig on the International Olympic Committee. He was heavily involved in sport, which Pam had no interest in.

She had a large majestic Irish setter named Big, old enough to have a few gray hairs on his muzzle. She said he liked to hide under the porch, pretending to protect his masters from aliens. Pam loved her Big to pieces.

I thought about my own dear Sunny, a collie-shepherd mix who some years ago, at the age of sixteen, was teleported to dog-heaven. My eyes leaked tears as I recalled what a loyal friend she had been, and such an uncomplaining foil in some of my books. I always gave her the best lines.

Pam told me she was currently taking a night course in psychology with a focus on Jung. It did occur to me that she was cozying up to me just to pick my brains, make better marks. Well, I didn't care one way or another. I was enamored. She could pick my brains clean to the bone; I'd try to do the same with her heart.

In my mind, then, I had a fantasy, an active imagination. It went something like this:

Pam snuggled up and breathed in my ear.

"Did you know it's unethical for a nurse to be intimate with the relative of a patient, even one as distant as you are?"

"I did not."

"Well it is."

"So?"

"So I'm bad."

"So I'm glad." I rubbed my fingers along her lips.

"But I'm also married," she said.

"A mere formality."

"Good evening, folks!" tinkled Pam. "This here is my husband, Mr. Formality! Please give him a round of applause!"

I had to laugh.

Pam said: "I guess that makes me badder than bad, eh?"

I thought of Jung's comment: "The good is always the enemy of the better. . . . If better is to come, good must stand aside."[20]

So what about the opposite—the bad and the worse? Now there's something to think about. I made another mental note. So much to think about! So little time!

"You're not alone," I said. "Partners often stay together long past the time when their relationship has ceased to be mutually satisfying. Why do you?"

"Oh, I don't know," Pam sighed. "Habit, I guess. Fear of the unknown, of being alone. Financial security. All that and a whole lot more. I like my husband, he's not a bad man. It's just that we don't have much in common any more."

"Well," I said, "the concept of individuation involves following your energy where it wants to go, and I guess it's no secret that I'm glad to receive yours."

Now there's a line as self-serving as Jung's view of adultery. I had the grace to blush.

Pam tickled my ribs and I almost lost my train of thought. I squirmed a safe distance away and continued.

"Of course in early life our energy is often pretty whimsical. We go with it willy-nilly because instinct rules the roost and we really don't know what else to do. We don't think much about the consequences

---

[20] "The Development of Personality," *The Development of Personality,* CW 17, par. 320.

either: babies! To some extent that's age appropriate, but it can get us into deep doo-doo."

"Yeah, I've been around that block," said Pam.

Me too, so I didn't need to pursue that.

"But bad can get worse," I said. "Later in life, burned by experience, we strive to be more conscious, more responsible, more aware of the consequences of following our energy, which, more than incidentally, might take us away from our current mate and, guess what, land us in even deeper doo-doo."

Pam's foot stroked my leg.

"Think of the scarab beetle," I said. "It pushes a ball of doo-doo in front of it. As the sacred Khepri, it was worshipped in ancient Egypt as the embodiment of the rising sun and of the creator god Atum. Khepri symbolized the self-regenerating life force. In Heliopolis this dung-beetle was seen as the god of transformation and symbol of the birth of the new sun from the womb of Mother Earth. How do you like that?"

Pam was silent for a time.

"That's pretty interesting," she said at last. "Maybe doo-doo of one kind or another is the essence of a meaningful life—one that at the end of it you can say, 'Sure, there was a lot of doo-doo, but it wasn't boring.' "

I kissed her nose. "I like that. Let's call it the Rolling Doo-Doo Theory, okay?"

"You talk a lot about doing," giggled Pam. "Maybe all your doing is just so much doo-doo!"

That hurt, but not too much. It was true enough that I do a lot more than I be. And I had never given much thought to how much of what I do is doo-doo. I tried meditation, but it didn't take; I kept thinking of what I might be doing instead. The only time I ever felt comfortable just being was many years ago when half the time I was stoned. I was happy as a lark doing nothing. But that didn't work either because it led to a midlife crisis and I lost my job and my girlfriend and I ran out of money to buy vegetables for my little ones. Then my wife left me and who could blame her?

But that was then and this was now. Lots of water under the bridge. I have some regrets, but not many. After wading through piles of doo-doo that to my mind were surely no less daunting than the heaps of manure Hercules faced in cleaning up the stables of Augeias—the sixth of his so-called Twelve Labors—I began to be myself. An essential aspect of the process of individuation is trial and error, and I don't need to blush about that.

I thought of Dr. Dolittle, the jolly veterinarian in kids' books who was devoted to caring for animals and laughed a lot. Now how did he get in here?

"Adam is such a sweetie," said Pam, pulling me close. "If he were your age I'd be with him instead. You know?"

"I guessed. Who could miss the way you fondled his chart?"

We rolled over and did it worse. Or maybe better, I'd lost track. I faintly heard music though.

Well, that was a fantasy, as I said. I'd been romancing my inner woman; let's call her Pam2. Thank goodness aural sex between us was not ethically proscribed. Sure, I had a few qualms about how Rachel might feel about this new fascination of mine, but on second thought I dismissed them because, when you get right down to it, Pam2 was really just another guise of Rachel herself.

Oh! I was suddenly dying for a smoke. For forty years I rolled my own and loved doing it, but then it became socially unacceptable and my doctor said don't be stupid, my kids said don't leave us, and every-thing I read spoke of an untimely demise if I continued to puff. So a few years ago I quit, and it was easier than I expected. Now, when I occasionally feel a craving, I think of a flock of birds passing over my head. I follow them with my eyes. Whoosh! Whoosh! And they're gone! And so is the craving! What can I say, it works.

I fell asleep with my arms wrapped around a teddy bear-elephant that I inherited from one of my daughters.

4
Batting the Ball with Nurse Pam

"Historically, did the ball come before the wheel?"

It was the real Pam speaking, a few days later. She was giving me a lavender jelly foot massage on the patio outside Adam's room. Adam was having his afternoon nap. Pam had made a pitcher of mint juleps, if you can stand it: Kentucky bourbon, crushed ice, fresh mint, sugar and tiny slices of lemon. It's a pretty good drink on a steamy hot day. We sucked it up through barber-shop straws.

"Hey," I said, "how would I know?"

See that? Call it my Adam complex.

Pam graced me with a coy smile.

"You are a psychoanalyst, you've written books. You know things others don't; well, me."

I was glad of the opportunity to set the record straight.

"It is true," I said, "that I have read a lot, but as a matter of fact, most of it I've forgotten. I've had more experience than some of those who come to me for analysis, and a whole lot less than others. I have some ideas in the back of my head, but they don't necessarily fit the person sitting in front of me What to do? I forget about theory and just listen. Often enough people solve their problems just by hearing themselves talk. Analysis is like surgery; you don't need it for a flesh wound."[21]

"You have an ingrown toe-nail," said Pam, pressing on it.

Ouch! I have read that a man's toe can indicate his way of life, his direction, and that the cutting off of thumbs and big toes was at one

---

[21] I learned that from Jung, who writes: "It would be a dangerous prejudice to imagine that analysis of the unconscious is the one and only panacea which should therefore be employed in every case. It is rather like a surgical operation and we should only resort to the knife when other methods have failed. So long as it does not obtrude itself the unconscious is best left alone." ("The Psychology of the Transference," *The Practice of Psychotherapy,* CW 16, par. 381)

time a Near-Eastern way of incapacitating a warrior. There is more, but not here.[22]

"Do that again and I'll pull your hair," I said crossly.

"Sorry," she smiled, "just having fun."

"I forgive you forever," I said.

In fact, it seemed to me that Pam's real fun lay in disturbing my wits—getting me to answer for who I was. She seemed genuinely interested in the substance, if any, behind my professional persona. I was becoming quite fond of her, and it occurred to me, not for the first time, how very easy it is to like someone who likes you.

Given time, I'm sure I could come up with plenty of personal associations and mythological amplifications to illuminate the psychological meaning of what was happening on Adam's patio. I mean, lavender jelly alone was probably good for two or three pages. And mint juleps, well, as much again if you include the Deep South and Blanche Dubois in *Streetcar Named Desire*.

As it was, however, I just felt happy to have a foot in Pam's receptive lap. Maybe that's as close to the state of being as I can ever get. The problem seems to be that it always feels like I'm playing hooky when I'm having fun instead of doing. So much to do! So little time! Of course there are also some things I have fun doing, but that's another story.

"In my personal life," I confessed, "I go in and out of the dark, just like anyone else. I have a few tools, like attending to my emotional reactions, listening to my dreams and talking to my inner others, but on the whole I'm quite befuddled."

"You're kidding me," smiled Pam.

"I am not. Listen, when I was in analysis in Zurich I dreamt of a spider skiing the slopes on a razor blade! And people say that the unconscious has no sense of humor! Well, I'm still working on that dream twenty-five years later."

Pam laughed. "I do like being with you."

"Ditto," I said, reaching across to hug her.

---

[22] See Ad de Vries, *Dictionary of Imagery and Symbolism,* p. 469.

We were breathless, not as if we had nothing more to say to each other, but rather too much.

"Modern life," I finally said, "has just about overtaken my capacity to deal with it. Computers? One more gigabyte and I'm done for. I have a mortgage, relationship problems, heart flutters. I have doubts. I forget more than I remember and I'm just as likely to be complexed as the next man—or woman. I'm not sexist, honest."

"So why," she teased, "would anyone pay good money to work with you as an analyst?"

I shrugged. "Maybe they'd be looking for something better. You know, there is a widespread misconception that an analyst's job is to help people. But our job is rather to better equip them to help themselves. I am little more than a midwife."

"Yeah, yeah," said Pam. "Hey! I almost forgot. The doo-doo fantasy you told me about? It took me to Simon & Garfunkle. They wrote a song that fits! Listen"—and she read from a scrap of paper:

Slow down, you're moving too fast,
you got to make the morning last,
just kicking down the cobblestones,
looking for fun and feeling groovy.

Ba da da da da da da, feeling groovy.

Hello lamppost, whatcha knowing?
I've come to watch your flowers growing.
Ain't ya got no rhymes for me?

Doo doo doo doo, feeling groovy.
Ba da da da da da da, feeling groovy.

I got no deeds to do, no promises to keep.
I'm dappled and drowsy and ready to sleep.
Let the morning time drop all its petals on me,
Life I love you, all is groovy.

Doo doo doo doo, feeling groovy.[23]

---

[23] "The 59th Street Bridge Song (Feelin' Groovy)," 1966.

"Kicking down the cobblestones!" she hooted. "I love it! Isn't that like following one's energy? And *dappled doo-doo,* isn't that synchronistic?!"

There, hear that? What is the difference between "kicking down the cobblestones" and "stumbling down the street tripping over bricks"? *Answer:* The former is characteristic of the imaginative intuitive mind, the latter of the prosaic sensation function. And the same for "dappled doo-doo" as opposed to "shady shit."

"Thanks for that," I laughed, "but feeling groovy ain't the same as individuating. One doesn't exclude the other, for sure, but feeling groovy can be an escape from adult responsibilities—you know, the puer/puella thing."

"No, I don't know," smiled Pam. "Think of me as your humble know-nothing reader."

Bless her, she was becoming quite as good a foil as Sunny. It became even clearer to me that my feeling for Pam had activated my creative muse, something like Toni Wolff did for Jung, or so it's said. Not that I identify with Jung. No, no, I'm not that inflated, but without a muse, inside or out, what do you have? Again, the big sleep.

I suddenly realized that balls and ball games had more to do with Eros than with Logos. I had something to say about that. The puer/puella thing could wait.

Out loud I said: "Pam, forgive me, it has just occurred to me that balls and ball games have more to do with Eros than with Logos. Do you mind?"

"Please," said Pam.

"In Greek mythology," I said, "Eros is the personification of love, a cosmogonic force of nature; psychologically it refers to the function of relationship. Logos is the principle of logic and structure, traditionally associated with spirit, the father world and the God-image. Both are symbolized by the attribute of light—Logos by the light of the sun and Eros by the light of the moon. In addition, Logos is associated with the right eye while Eros is related to the left eye.

"Jung had quite a lot to say about these concepts. In his earlier writings, he equated Logos with the conscious principle of man, and

Eros with the conscious principle of woman. He was roundly criticized for this. He responded":

> By Logos I meant discrimination, judgment, insight, and by Eros I meant the capacity to relate. I regarded both concepts as intuitive ideas which cannot be defined accurately or exhaustively. From the scientific point of view this is regrettable, but from a practical one it has its value, since the two concepts mark out a field of experience which it is equally difficult to define.[24]

You have to admire the way Jung got out of a tough spot by tying himself up in knots. Even Houdini never tried that.

"Of course," I said to Pam, "Jung acknowledged that either Eros or Logos could be dominant in any particular man or woman. There are men who can't discriminate well and their judgment's not so good, but they relate to others; you feel good when you're with them. I know men like that; day-care workers, therapists of one kind or another, social workers, cab drivers, whatever. And there are women who bungle their relationships but score high in the Logos area. You can find them in the professions or running their own business. They can be very efficient and competent in what they do, but like me they have difficulty in just being."

Pam asked: "Did Jung actually believe that a man's most natural way of functioning was through Logos?"

"Well, he saw that as the archetypal truth. A man might not be good at it—discriminating, differentiating and so on—but yes, Jung thought that was a man's natural biological bent."

"And if a man doesn't function like that at all?"

"Well, theoretically it could be that his ideas and behavior patterns are overly influenced by his feminine side, his anima."

"That would be what you call anima-possession?"

So, she didn't know nothing after all. Crafty. I bet she knows something about animus too.

"In the extreme, yes," I said. "But of course how that manifests

---

[24] *Mysterium Coniunctionis,* CW 14, par. 224.

would depend on a number of things. If his inner woman was overly identified with the mother—which is often the case—our hypothetical gent would defer to the women in his life, find it difficult to say No. In case of a conflict, he wouldn't put up a fight; he'd back off, agree, apologize, placate, hide his feelings under a bushel—anything to make things right. At the drop of a hat he'd be sentimental, completely identified with his emotions."

"He'd be a wimp?" asked Pam.

"As a matter of fact," I said, "he might very well be a jock. But typically he'd be irritable, moody and oversensitive. Behind all that is the mother complex. Whether a man's experience of his personal mother was good or bad, he carries the complex inside for his whole life. One way or another it will always color his relationships."

"Poor guys," she said, with no trace of sarcasm.

I pressed on.

"Now, for a woman—according to Jung—*her* conscious way of functioning, archetypally grounded in the principle of Eros, is colored by the unconscious influence of her animus—an inner masculine voice that is often very critical and judgmental. And if she were dominated by a negative animus—which would mean she was out of touch with Eros, her 'natural' feminine nature—we'd call her animus-possessed. In business she'd play hardball, just like a mean-spirited man."

"A ball-breaker?"

"Well, that's the way a man might experience her. Maybe she'd just have more balls than he did."

"Wouldn't his mother complex play a part?"

"For sure. A man's reactions to a woman always involve his mother complex, just as a woman's response to a man is determined by her father complex."

Pam grimaced, masking her usual cheerful smile.

Oops! a button I wouldn't have knowingly pushed. I suddenly realized how little I knew of her life, her schooling, ambitions and the like. Selfish me. I vowed that one day we would talk only about her.

Pam gave away nothing more personal, saying: "Okay, what if a woman has a positive father complex?"

"Ah, well," I said, "she would be very lucky in some ways, but not so in others. She'd be what we call a father's daughter, his 'little princess,' who from an early age functions as his connection to an inner reality, but, sorry to say, often at the expense of her own psychological development."[25]

She was still fondling my foot and it felt so good I wanted to hug her to bits, but I wasn't quite finished.

"In his later writing on alchemy," I said, "Jung described Logos and Eros as psychologically equivalent to solar and lunar consciousness, archetypal ideas analogous to the Eastern concepts of yang and yin— again, opposite but complementary kinds of energy.[26]

"Yang, the masculine, is associated with *doing*—penetrating, incisive action—and yin, the feminine, with *being*—everything we associate with passive and receptive. This didn't change Jung's view that Eros is more specific, more natural, to feminine consciousness and Logos to masculine consciousness. And so he still attributed Eros in a man to the influence of the anima, and Logos in a woman to the influence of the animus. He expressed it like this":

> In a man it is the lunar anima, in a woman the solar animus, that influences consciousness in the highest degree. Even if a man is often unaware of his own anima-possession, he has, understandably enough, all the more vivid an impression of the animus-possession of his wife, and vice versa.[27]

"And there you have it in a nutshell," I said, as if that were the final word.

Just then Adam buzzed for attention. Pam was off in a flash. I followed her in. He had kicked his covers off and his bony little body was all askew.

"There now," soothed Pam, putting things right. "it's okay, I'm here. How do you feel?"

---

[25] See Marion Woodman, *The Pregnant Virgin: A Process of Psychological Transformation,* esp. pp. 35ff.

[26] See Richard Wilhelm, trans., *The I Ching or Book of Changes,* Hexagrams 1 and 2.

[27] *Mysterium Coniunctionis,* CW 14, par. 225.

Adam groaned. "I dreamt I was tarred and feathered by the witch of the east."

"Maybe you oughta be," I joked, thinking that sometimes dreams mean what they say. But I was not inclined to try to understand this one, since it would mean asking Adam for his associations to tar and feathers and the witch of the east, not to mention what he had for breakfast and what had been on his mind before he fell asleep. There are those who say they can interpret dreams without knowing such mundane details, but I'm at a loss without them. And so, in general, was Jung himself.[28]

Pam clucked and Adam mumbled himself back to never-never land. Pam and I went back to the dappled patio.

"You were going to tell me about puers," she said, topping up our juleps. "Here, gimme your other foot."

And she got out the lavender jelly.

My mind was busy. Feet symbolize one's standpoint, one's place in the world. I once dreamt that I was hobbling about on stumps, juggling chocolate Hershey heart-drops. I was grateful for that image. It expressed rather well where I was at the time: no personal standpoint, dependent on sweethearts of one kind and another, none of whom provided true nourishment. Of course, a foot in a lovely's lap could escalate to something more—if her hands roved to my knee, say, or maybe even higher—thinking of which, I recalled that according to some ancient philosophers, like Plutarch and Pliny, the knees are the seat of a man's life-force, his strength.[29] I didn't say that out loud.

"Well," I said, "there's not a lot to say about puers that hasn't been said by the late doyenne of Jungian analysts, Marie-Louise von Franz. She's the expert, but others have had some good insights on the subject too."[30]

---

[28] See "On the Nature of Dreams," *The Structure and Dynamics of the Psyche,* CW 8, pars. 533ff.

[29] See R.B. Onians, *The Origins of European Thought,* pp. 185ff.

[30] See von Franz, *The Problem of the Puer Aeternus;* also Ann Yeoman, *Now or Neverland: Peter Pan and the Myth of Eternal Youth.*

"I'd like to hear your take on it," coaxed Pam.

I was sorely tempted. I did so like having her play with my feet, and even if there had been no erotic charge between us I was not immune to showing off. However, I had a client due in half an hour, so there just wasn't time.

"Will you take a rain-check?" I asked.

"For sure," she smiled, wiping off the excess jelly.

I went home in such terrific spirits that after my analytic hour and a tasty dinner featuring Luigi's succulent shepherd's pie—ground sirloin, minced onions, creamed corn and honey mustard—with a side salad of romaine lettuce, celery hearts and radicchio, I spent the evening sipping Scotch and working on my manuscript.

Thinking of what I was writing, I kept bouncing back and forth between the opposites. On the one hand it was a masterpiece, right up there with *Doctor Zhivago* or *War and Peace;* on the other hand it was a self-indulgent piece of shite.

My mind drifted to wondering what goes on in one's head in writing a book. There are theories, but nobody really knows. The only sure thing is that there are as many different ways to write as there are writers. Some say they till the ground, plant the seed and watch it grow. For me it's like assembling a patchwork quilt. I have the patches; it's the needles that give me a hard time.

Jung had something to say on the subject. Of course he didn't *know* either, but he had some ideas. Here is his basic standpoint:

> The practice of art is a psychological activity and, as such, can be approached from a psychological angle. . . . This statement, however, involves a very definite limitation of the psychological viewpoint when we come to apply it in practice. Only that aspect of art which consists in the process of artistic creation can be a subject for psychological study, but not that which constitutes its essential nature. The question of what art is in itself can never be answered by the psychologist, but must be approached from the side of aesthetics.[31]

---

[31] "On the Relation of Analytical Psychology to Poetry," *The Spirit in Man, Art, and Literature,* CW 15, par. 97.

I understood Jung to be saying that the process of creating is a legitimate subject for psychological speculation. But psychology can't determine whether the end result is art or not. That depends on contemporary taste.

Closer to home, I wondered how I came to be putting energy into this self-styled romance. It had me by the throat, that's for sure. I found these further comments by Jung:

> The unborn work in the psyche of the artist is a force of nature that achieves its end either with tyrannical might or with the subtle cunning of nature herself. . . We would do well, therefore, to think of the creative process as a living thing implanted in the human psyche. In the language of analytical psychology this living thing is an *autonomous complex*. It is a split-off portion of the psyche, which leads a life of its own outside the hierarchy of consciousness. Depending on its energy charge, it may appear either as a mere disturbance of conscious activities or as a supraordinate authority which can harness the ego to its purpose.[32]

Aha, so it is a complex that drives me to create! I could live with that, even enjoy it. I fell asleep feeling that the process was more important than the end result. And so, if what I was writing was only worth something to myself, that was okay too.

Rachel appeared that night in a dream. I woke up with an image of her in overalls and suspenders, her hair in pig-tails, like Dorothy in *The Wizard of Oz*.

"I've been to a blue-collar wedding and a hoo-haw barn dance," she said. "I fell head over heels for a gee-whiz hayseed!"

That was too much for me.

"Good for you," I said, and went back to sleep.

---

[32] Ibid., par. 115.

5
On Growing Up

It was a late afternoon in mid-October. I was restless. I had so much on my plate that my head was in a whirl. Old friends were dying or getting married. Some of my kids were buying houses, others were about to have babies. I was going to be a grandfather, which I'd probably get used to, but still.

At the nursing home I paid my respects to Adam, who just went on snoring. Anyway, I was there to have some time with Pam. It was too chilly for the patio, so after she arranged for a colleague to spell her we took off to the Starbucks around the corner. We nursed our lattes, pretending we were on official business in case anyone gave a hoot, which I doubted, but of course Pam liked to maintain some cover for our get-togethers.

"Last night," said Pam, "in the course I'm taking? There was a lot of talk about how do you know where you are in the process of your psychological development."

"Yes," I said, "that is a good question."

I ground my teeth, which is what I usually do when I don't know what to say next.

"Well?" said Pam.

She was so comely; there was a delightfully numinous aura about her, I could hardly stand it.[33]

"There's no one answer," I said. "It's largely subjective, so it can't be answered theoretically. Have you thought of seeing an analyst?"

That was uncalled for, and none of my business anyway, but it's what I said. Sometimes things just pop out.

---

[33] "Numinous: Descriptive of persons, things or situations having a deep emotional resonance, psychologically associated with experiences of the Self. Numinous, like numinosity, comes from Latin *numinosum,* referring to a dynamic agency or effect independent of the conscious will." (Sharp, *Jung Lexicon,* p. 92)

Pam didn't flinch.

"Listen," she said, "maybe one day I will, but I'm just not there yet and I can't afford it now anyway. In the meantime, please, I would like some guidelines, some parameters, something to hold on to."

I swallowed.

"Well, we could pick up on the puer/puella thing."

"I would like that," smiled Pam. "I think it would be preferable to sitting here making small talk when we'd rather be making love."

I could not have expressed it better.

"Okay," I said, gathering my thoughts. "In Jungian psychology the term puer is used to describe an adult man whose emotional life has remained at an adolescent level, usually coupled with too great a dependence on the mother. The term puella is used for a woman, though we also speak of a woman with a puer animus—a father's daughter. The puer/puella syndrome is not an issue in one's early years, because the symptoms then are age-appropriate, but many psychological crises in later life arise from the inner need to grow up.

"The expression *puer aeternus* is Latin for eternal boy. In Greek mythology it designates a child-god who is forever young, like Iacchus, Dionysus, Eros. The theme is immortalized in the modern classics *Peter Pan* and *The Picture of Dorian Gray*. The typical puer doesn't look his age and is proud of it. Who would not be, in our Western culture where youth is worshipped?"

"Isn't there something to be said for working out, keeping fit?" countered Pam. "That's what all the health books say."

"Indeed," I said. "I do yoga twice a week myself, and walk an hour a day. Exercise? Do it. But face-lifts? Hair transplants? Liposuction? No thanks. Of course, any man would be shocked at the suggestion that his youthful appearance is due to emotional immaturity. So would a woman."

"Hey!" said Pam. "You look younger than your years!"

"So I'm emotionally immature! At least I know it."

As if that made it okay. Jeez, I can even con myself.

"As well," I added, "following the psychological rule of projection—that we see in others traits of our own that we're unconscious of—women who fall head over heels for puers are themselves quite likely to be puellas. And, as it happens, vice versa."

"Do you think I could fall for a puer?" asked Pam.

I eyed her. For sure she had some characteristics of a puella, but she wasn't only that.

"I don't know," I said. "Maybe you're a hybrid, nicely balanced on the razor's edge, so to speak; you like to play but you're not irresponsible, so you don't let the ball run you over."

Pam laughed and I went on.

"The typical puer shirks responsibility for his actions, and understandably so, since what he does is not within his conscious control. He is at the mercy of the unconscious, and is especially vulnerable to his instinctive drives. He is prone to do what feels right. But he's so alienated from his true feelings that what feels right one minute often feels wrong the next. So, for instance, he may find himself in erotic situations that cause him a good deal of distress the next day—or that night, in his dreams."

"Ball dreams?" asked Pam.

"Yeah, maybe, like the one that took me into analysis."

But I wasn't yet ready to talk about that. Some things you can tell anybody, some you can only tell close friends, and there's a lot you have to keep absolutely private until the time is right. Oh, and there are some things you don't even tell yourself.

"Anyway," I said, "the individuating puer—one coming to grips with his attitudes and behavior patterns—knows that undifferentiated feelings are highly suspect, especially when they arise in conjunction with the use of alcohol or other drugs. Instead of identifying with his feelings, he tries to keep some distance from them, which means objectifying what he's experiencing. He questions himself: Is this me? Is this what I really feel? Is this what I want? What are the consequences? Can I live with them? Can I live with myself? How does what I do affect others?"

"I like that," said Pam. "What else?"

"Puers generally have a hard time with commitment," I said. "They like to keep their options open and can't bear to be tied down.

They act spontaneously, with little thought of how they affect others. The individuating puer must acknowledge all that and give it up— but what he sacrifices then becomes part of his shadow. Later in life, in order then not to be ruled by habit and routine, he may have to re-assimilate—this time consciously—his lapsed puer traits."

"I bet that's you!" cried Pam.

I tried to look sheepish. It was a fact that lately I'd been frequenting my old Dionysian haunts—pubs, jazz joints and so on, dancing till the wee hours, drinking more than usual, flirting like crazy, the whole ball of wax. I didn't say that, though. Like I said, some things you have to keep to yourself on account of your personal temenos.

"And what else?" she asked.

"Well, also symptomatic of puer psychology is the feeling of being special, of having a unique destiny. When you feel like that it's hard to muster the energy to earn a living. Compared to what you're cut out for, the daily grind is just too mundane. This is a variety of inflation. You feel special, so why, you wonder, are you doing something so ordinary?"

I paused to catch my breath.

"If this attitude persists," I said, "you can cheerfully rationalize wasting your life, waiting for destiny to catch up or fall from the sky. You play the lotteries, the track, the slots, and you buy stocks. You know the odds are against you but you cross your fingers and hope you'll win, and you hedge your bets with options and silver futures."

Pam shook her head.

"Boy oh boy, I know guys like that, and a few women too."

"Listen," I said, "my favorite aunt, my mother's sister Marge, was a puella. As a grown woman she sat by the window for hours, gazing at the horizon. 'One day,' she would sigh, 'my ship will come in.' She lived in a small town on the prairies, a thousand miles from any sea. Her husband, a frail reed of a man, worked his whole life on an assembly line in a brewery, filling one bottle after another, day after day, drinking spillovers, dreaming of being the brewmaster."

Pam smiled. "You made that up!"

"If only I could," I said. "Then I'd write novels. Those are true facts. My Auntie Marge and Uncle Sid were kindly folks, I loved them both. It is only in retrospect that I see them psychologically as prime examples of the provisional life. You see, puers and puellas are always about to make a change; one day they'll do what's necessary—but not just yet. They are awash in a world of maybes: 'Maybe I'll do this . . . maybe that . . .' Plans for the future come to nothing; life slips away in fantasies of what will be, what could be, while nothing is done to change the here and now."

"Sounds like a kind of prison to me," said Pam.

"And so it is," I nodded. "A prison in which the bars are the parental complexes, unconscious ties to early life, the boundless irresponsibility of the child. I can tell you, the dreams of puers and puellas are full of prison imagery: chains, bars, cages, entrapment, bondage. I've had dozens of such dreams myself! Life itself, reality as puers find it, is experienced as imprisonment. They yearn for independence and long for freedom, but they're powerless to pull it off."

Pam tsk-tsked.

"Listen to this," I said, pulling a book from my knapsack. "Here's von Franz's description of the prison phobia of a young mother-bound man":

> The prison is the negative symbol of the mother-complex . . . or it would be prospectively just exactly what he needs, for he needs to be put into prison, into the prison of reality. But if he runs away from the prison of reality, he is in the prison of his mother complex, so it is prison anyway, wherever he turns. He has only the choice of two prisons, either that of his neurosis or that of his reality; thus he is caught between the devil and the deep blue sea. That is his fate, and that is the fate of the *puer aeternus* altogether. It is up to him which he prefers: that of his mother complex and his neurosis, or of being caught in the just-so story of earthly reality.[34]

Pam was wide-eyed.

Oh, I did like to wow her with insider stuff she wouldn't likely get from her Jung 101 night course.

---

[34] *The Problem of the Puer Aeternus*, p. 134.

"Puers typically chafe at boundaries and limits," I went on. "They tend to view any restriction as intolerable. They don't realize that some limits are indispensable for growth. It's a lucky puer or puella whose unconscious eventually rebels and makes its dissatisfaction apparent through a psychological crisis. Otherwise you stay stuck and shallow. The big sleep."

"So," said Pam, wrinkling her adorable nose, "what's the alternative?"

"Growing up." I said. "You see, the puer's opposite number, his shadow, is the senex—Latin for old man. In Western culture, a senex man is traditionally seen as disciplined, conscientious, well organized, goal oriented. Similarly, the shadow of the senex is the puer: unbounded instinct, disordered, intoxicated, whimsical. You can see the puer's mythological counterpart most clearly in the Greek god Dionysus, whose female followers—puella acolytes, I like to call them— ripped men to pieces in an erotic frenzy. Senex psychology is appropriately characterized by Saturn and the god Apollo: conservative, rational, responsible—dull!

"Senex men do their duty, count their money and are home for dinner. Senex women are there to cook for them, even if it's only macaroni and cheese."

Pam smiled. "Sounds pretty boring."

"Could be," I said. "If you're all senex you don't have a ball at all; life is all work and no play. But few men or women are only that, or only puer or puella either. Real life is an ongoing matter of mix and match. We all have our psychological priorities and behavior patterns, the way we mostly are, but usually we make room for the opposite. If we don't, we become sad and depressed."

Pam yawned. So maybe she wasn't wowed, just tired. I pretended not to notice.

"You've probably heard it said that the passage of time turns liberals into conservatives. Likewise, puers and puellas become old men and women, and, if they have learned from their experience, possibly even wise. But at any stage of life we have to make a place for both puer and senex. It's a matter of balance. In fact, whoever lives one pattern exclusively risks constellating the opposite. Enantiodromia is waiting in the wings: the more one-sided we are, the more likely it is that the opposite will break through to turn our lives around."

"And what is that—enantiodromia?" asked Pam.

"Jung defined it as the emergence or activation of the unconscious opposite in the course of time.[35] Like St. Paul's conversion on the road to Damascus."

"Paul was a misogynist," frowned Pam.

"Was he?"

You could put my knowledge of the founding Church Fathers in a tea cup. One thing I did know about Pam was that she was brought up by fundamentalist born-again Christians. In place of Mom and Dad she'd had Mary and Joseph. Powerful parental images, but in time she rebelled against them, just as we all do and apparently must.[36]

"It all sounds so complicated," she sighed. "How does one know what to think, what to do, how to be?"

As if I knew.

When I was a young man, I was concerned to figure out where and how I might fit into the larger picture, how to make a mark. I had a fantasy that somewhere there was a big book of collective wisdom that contained prescribed solutions to all life's problems. Whenever you found yourself in a quandary you could just look it up in *The Big Book* and do what it said. (In my mind's eye it had a really good index, too.) If there was a book like that, I wouldn't have to think for myself. I'd just do what was laid down by tradition. Such a fantasy is symptomatic of a father complex.

All the same, I was not above offering Pam some suggestions. When someone thinks you are as wise as you're not, it is hard to resist pontificating. I mean sure, there's a limit, but I wasn't even close to it yet.

"Introspection, trial and error," I intoned. "Careful consideration of your ups and downs, your dreams and conflicts, emotional reactions

---

[35] "Definitions," *Psychological Types,* CW 6, par. 709.

[36] See M. Esther Harding, *The Parental Image: Its Injury and Reconstruction.*

to other people. I think of it like this: A healthy, well-balanced personality is capable of functioning according to what is appropriate at any given time. Of course that's the ideal, seldom attained without a conscious effort to get to know yourself."

Pam nodded.

"As a matter of fact," I continued, "personal analysis quite as often involves the need for a well-controlled senex person to reconnect with the spontaneous, instinctual life, as it does the puer's need to grow up. It's all tied in with the process of individuation. You follow your energy and take your chances. But it's not a matter of win or lose. It's your life. You win just by living it, and if you keep your wits about you, you also get to have a relationship with the Self, your regulating center."

I took a breath and continued.

"Marie-Louise von Franz says that having a relationship with the Self is like being in touch with an instinct of truth. There's an immediate awareness of what is right and true for you, a bone-deep truth without reflection."[37]

Pam was quiet. So was I.

After a few minutes Pam surfaced to say: "If life isn't a ball, is it a game? And if it's a game, is it a ball? And if it isn't a game, just what are we playing at?"

Good questions. I didn't have answers.

She blew her nose and stuffed the tissue back in her sleeve.

"My husband is definitely senex," she said. Her eyes welled up. "The big sleep. Psychology? Getting to know himself? Forget it. But we're attached. We get along okay, and all in all we have a pretty good life. So I'm not about to run off with some Don Juan, however charming—oh yes you are, don't deny it!"

Well, right enough, I am also that. It's only if she'd said "nothing but" that would get my back up.

"I would like to have my cake and eat it too," said Pam, "stay with him on the surface, for good or for better, for bad or for worse, and be

---

[37] See *Alchemy: An Introduction to the Symbolism and the Psychology,* pp. 172f.

with you as your top-secret *anam cara*."

"My what?"

"*Anam cara,* that's Gaelic for soul friend. I read it in a book."[38]

I smiled.

"So," said Pam, "here's what I'm saying, I will be your loverNot if you will be mine. How's that?"

LoverNot! What a mind.

"Puella to puer," I mused. "It could work."

"Tell me true," she said. "Could you hold the tension?"

Well, I wasn't at all sure. I would certainly have a conflict.

"Tell you what," I said. "I'll try not to get my balls in an uproar."

"Me too," smiled Pam and skipped off, back to Adam.

In bed that night I reminded myself of what is involved in the sparkles between a man and a woman, and how psychologically salutary it can be for them to acknowledge the mutual attraction but refrain from acting it out.

Given that the man's anima and the woman's animus are always involved in the attraction via projection—each being a reasonably good hook for what is dormant in the other—not concretizing the relationship is a good opportunity for them to get to know their inner contrasexual sides. That's classical Jungian theory, which I am inclined to accept, not exactly as Gospel, no no—though the spiritual implications do not escape me—but in general I think it is a reasonable working hypothesis.

Of course, you can act out the attraction anyway and take your lumps. God knows I've done that often enough. But this was somehow different. I respected Pam's situation and I was willing to put desire on the shelf in favor of what she meant to me psychologically. That meant keeping close track of my reactions to her, my moods and so on. Perhaps she would do the same. And if the urge to get our feet wet became overwhelming, we could always take a cold shower.

Only not together.

---

[38] See John O'Donohue, *Anam Cara: A Book of Celtic Wisdom.*

6
The Heart as Lonely Hunter

Time passed. I saw Adam often enough; we had some great laughs plotting our next caper. And Pam too; one way or another we were together several times a month—at the nursing home, my house or art shows, downtown walks, occasionally a movie or a restaurant. The winter was unseemly harsh, so cold that my hydrangeas and euonymous were in tatters. And then suddenly it was spring, with flowers everywhere.

One breezy Saturday morning in May I woke up feeling alone and old. I shaved and my father's face in the mirror shaved back at me. That didn't help. Gray hairs in my nose! Liver spots! Wrinkles! How disgusting. It's enough to drive me back to Beckett. My voice was hoarse, as if I'd gargled razor blades. Soon I'd be Adam's age. I didn't like the thought. My father in the mirror said I'd better get used to it.

I was curt with Luigi because there was no orange juice. And he burnt the friggin' toast!

So I have a toast complex, I'm not perfect.

Walking down to the post office these days, I notice older women more than I used to. I mean those around my own age, senior citizens if you're counting. When one smiles at me, I smile back and wonder what her life is like. Married? Children? What is her work? What goes on in her head? Is she lonely? Does she wonder who she is, really? Is she sexually active?[39] As they used to say in the fifties when introducing that radio program *Dragnet*, "There are a million stories in the city." Well, mine is one of them and so are theirs.

---

[39] I don't mean to be coarse, but sensation types are typically more interested in the body than the soul. And anyway, Western culture is so obsessed with youth that the *cognoscenti*, those in the know, need to trumpet the sex appeal of older women. I think I could write a book about that, but probably I won't. So much else to do, so little time.

So many fantasies. So much unlived life.

Over a bowl of porridge and raisins, lightly sugared, with just a touch of cinnamon and a teaspoon of chopped nuts, I thought of various lovelies at hand, and especially of the good Nurse Pam. Well, she herself wasn't actually at hand. She had gone to Nassau to be by the ocean for a couple of weeks.

But before she left, Pam came over to hang out for an afternoon by my pool. She told me how she looked forward to her time away from her usual routine, and how she loved being near the majesty of surf and rocks, waves and sand.

"I will spend long hours alone," she said, "walking, dreaming, thinking. Some of my most inspirational moments and insights have occurred by the sea. I have grieved, longed, sung, run and felt joy at the sea. I have it in my blood, I guess."

It was unseasonably warm and we dipped in and out to cool off. Pam looked terrific in her two-piece bathing suit.

"Hey, you're not very tall, are you," I said innocently, as if I hadn't rehearsed it a dozen times.

"Well no, but I try to be," she smiled.[40] We hugged.

I showed her what I'd been working on. She got quite excited.

"Wow, you're going a mile a minute!" she said.

Then she popped me a riddle. "What is a razor on a roll? Come on!" she laughed. "Think sideways! *What is a razor on a roll?*"

My mind searched. I could only think of Oedipus' answer to the Sphinx's question ("What goes on four legs in the morning, on two at noon, and on three in the evening?")[41] but that didn't seem to fit. I

---

[40] This was Bogey's quip-reply to the pouty nymphet's come-on/put-down in the opening scene of *The Big Sleep*. So, Pam had seen the film too. (I was just checking.)

[41] Oedipus answered: "Man, who crawls as a child, walks erect in manhood, and uses a cane in old age." Jung thought that missed the point: "The riddle was, in fact, the trap which the Sphinx laid for the unwary wanderer. Overestimating his intellect in a typically masculine way, Oedipus walked right into it, and unknowingly committed the crime of incest [i.e., later marrying his mother Jocasta]. The riddle of the Sphinx was *herself*—the terrible mother-imago, which Oedipus would not take as a warning." (*Symbols of Transformation*, CW 5, par. 265)

guessed wildly: "Sharp old cheddar, with hot chili peppers and freckled Dijon mustard on an onion bun . . . with a slice of sour pickle?!"

"Roller blade!" she cried.

Now there's a whimsical imagination. If I could think like that I'd be . . . well, someone else.

"On the other hand," frowned Pam, "you aren't writing much about balls."

It was an innocent remark, but I was immediately defensive. Like I said earlier, being called on what I don't do right, or what I might have done wrong, is one of my buttons. Maybe that derives from not getting enough mother's milk, being switched to a bottle too soon. Or when I was eight years old in Grade Three and the prissy Ms. Bishop rapped my knuckles with a ruler for holding hands with my seatmate Janet Kowalski, who I had promised to marry. Or perhaps it's because I got tripped up on "onomatopoeia" in a Grade Five spelling bee. Well, whatever, I sure wasn't about to spend a few years in Freudian analysis to find out.

"But I am, I am," I said to Pam. "It's just that much of it is *sotto voce*. In case you haven't noticed, balls of one kind or another permeate this book."

That was pushing the truth, but again, think about it: if I didn't, who would?

"And ball games?" she teased.

"Yes, that was in the outline," I acknowledged, "but then I conferred with Adam. And then I met you. What can I say? I've changed my focus. I've moved on to bigger and better things. Now I'm exploring why I *don't* think the world is a turd!—and just trying to get my head around that is changing my life. Maybe yours too. Feel the wind, the breeze on your back, the tug at your heart? I'm your lover-Not, yes, but I am also, implicitly, your lover-in-waiting. And it really doesn't matter if that never happens."

I breathed easy.

"Do you see? I'm your typical, simple-minded fairy-tale Dummling who wins the treasure because he doesn't know any better. He doesn't give up, he just does the next thing in front of him and before you

know it he has a sack of gold or he's in bed with the princess or van-
quishes the evil witch, whatever; it all comes down to the same thing,
namely that he gets to know himself a little better."

And I call myself an introvert, just like everyone else who with-
draws from the hurly-burly of life for an hour or two a week to wonder what they're doing.

"And by the way," I said, "can you winkle an evening free for dinner and a movie?"

Pam frowned. "It's not so easy . . ."

I didn't push it.

Pam brightened.

"I've been browsing in your Brillig Trilogy," she said. "Adam lent
me the books. He pretended they were nothing, just a bauble—that's
what he said—but I think he's very proud of them."

"Oh?" As if I didn't know.

"You two were pretty close then, weren't you?"

"Well, we sure had some fun."

I had to arm-wrestle him at times, but still.

"They're not only fun to read," said Pam. "There's a serious sub-
text and a strange kind of tension. I think they're quite wonderful!
You humanize analysis—you present it as an encounter between
grown-ups. You take the mystique out of the process. You give people
like me hope. You speak with authority, but just when your reader—
well, me at least—thinks you're about to give the answer to life, you
and Adam are off on another romp! Last night I laughed myself to
sleep. I hope you write another."

I blushed. "You are a very generous woman. I inflate myself with
false modesty."

"Better than being ball'd, like Adam!" squealed Pam.

Ball'd, bald. There she goes again. Now what can you do with
goofiness like that? Especially when your own inclination is to ar-
range groceries in the cupboard alphabetically: Beans, Bread, Cereal,
Coffee, Corn, Honey, Jam, Noodles, Oil, Peanut Butter, Peas, Pep-
percorns, Salt, Soup, Spaghetti, Spices, and so on. And you can never
get it right on account of all the subcategories and arbitrary deci-

sions—does a tin of pork and beans go under P or B? balsamic vinaigrette under B or V?—and even if you could you'd soon run out of shelves. It's a mug's game, I can tell you. And if on top of that you have an irresistible desire to straighten the pictures on other people's walls . . . well, don't get me started.

So, you can either scoff at whimsy and go your less-than-merry way, or you can welcome the fun, even appreciate it. I chose the latter, and why not? You don't get far romancing a lovely by ridiculing the way she thinks.

I took Pam's hands in mine. Long, delicate fingers. Well-kept nails with scarlet polish. I tried not to think of them raking my back in the throes of unrestrained passion. We had made a pact and I meant to honor it. I was concerned to be a good boy, to adhere to what is known these days in academic psychology as "intelligent behavior." That's where you don't simply respond to a person or a situation automatically, instinctively. In simple language, you don't act out. In other words, I would pretend to be a grown-up as long as I could.

Pam was smiling. She disengaged one of her hands from mine and took one of mine in hers. She raised it to her lips. Such a romantic gesture, I almost fell over. I thought she was going to say something, but she didn't; she just went on smiling.

Oh! I was beginning to believe she really liked me. You see, the shadow side of a positive mother complex is the feeling that you are an imposter and not lovable at all . . .

"The fact is," I said, "I have nothing new to say. I embroider, I stitch and sew. I am not an original thinker. I steal shamelessly from Jung and others. But I have to write, call it an addiction if you like, a compulsion, or even substance abuse. Do you know what? When I was in Grade Seven a teacher praised me for a paper I wrote on Shakespeare's *All's Well That Ends Well.* I guess I took it to heart."

"Come now," smiled Pam.

"It's true," I said. "The urge to express myself is what gets me up in the morning. Of course I love working with a few analysands, but finding a new container for promoting the practical application of Jung's ideas—that's what really gets me rolling. I don't know, maybe that's why I got interested in balls in the first place, what with them containing the greatest amount of stuff relative to their surface area."

"I see," nodded Pam. "Compact, but jam-packed inside?"

"I like to think so, though I'm not so sure about the jam. Peach? Grape? Strawberry? Pearl?"

Pam was in stitches, go figure.

"Okay," I said, "to use another metaphor, from time to time the gods favor me with a bone that I worry to death—get all the meat off, and then keep on gnawing till maybe I might crack through to the rich marrow. Well, that's what Sunny used to do, or so she said."

"Big does that too," sighed Pam.

I kissed her well and wished her a safe journey.

She clung to me, as I to her.

"Do you love me?" asked Pam.

I searched for what to say. For the past few days I had been listening over and over to Frank Sinatra, ol' blue eyes himself, singing love songs. The lyrics to "Somethin' Stupid" stuck in my head:

I know I stand in line
Until you think you have the time
to spend an evening with me.

And if we go some place to dance,
I know there's a chance
you won't be leaving with me.

And afterwards we drop into a quiet place
and have a drink or two.
And then I go and spoil it all by saying
Somethin' stupid like "I love you."[42]

I was bursting to say the L-word, but I didn't want to overplay my hand—I mean, pretend I had a straight or a full house when I only held three Jacks, a two and a five.

As a matter of fact, I am your confirmed gamblerNot. When I was in my early twenties a friend coerced me to accompany him to the

---

[42] Lyrics by Carson C. Parks.

race track, where I lost more than I could afford. I haven't bet on anything since; well, other than a couple of years ago when that same friend got me drunk in an Irish pub and dared me to describe the color of my socks without looking. I lost that time too, though not more than I could afford.

Finally I said: "No, but I think I could. I don't generally fall in love with a woman before going to bed with her. Until then I'm just your common and garden-variety loose cannon."

"Keep your powder dry," Pam smiled. "I'm comin' back."

She donned her *French Lieutenant's Woman* cape and left. She paused at the sidewalk to look back, as she always did. She waved and blew me a kiss. . . .

Ah! my heart was so full of her that I had to support myself. In my head I heard Rod Stewart:

> *No tears, no fears,*
> *Remember, there's always tomorrow.*
> *So what if we have to part*
> *We'll be together again*
>
> *Try thinking with your heart,*
> *We'll be together again.*[43]

I would miss Pam, but of course I'd still have her stand-in, Pam2, so I didn't think I'd be all that lonely. After all, Pam2 has many qualities that I project onto the real Pam, who is only marginally who I think she is anyway. But then again, if the real Pam didn't have some characteristics of Pam2 I wouldn't be interested in her at all, would I? Or maybe I would anyway; perhaps, possibly.

I wish I knew everything, but I don't.

After a few minutes of feeling disorientated, which always happens when Pam and I part, I roused myself and put on a CD of baroque violin concertos, Bach and Vivaldi.

In short order I was enveloped by the ineffable and didn't give a fig for anything else.

---

[43] Lyrics by Carl Fischer and Frankie Laine.

7
Love's Labor Lost

The day after Pam left I awoke in a foul mood. I moped around till noon. I couldn't settle, didn't feel like writing. I wonderfully thought of Pam. If she were not out there, I would have to invent her, which thankfully I didn't have to do because she *was* out there! . . . And also *in here!* That is called being in two places at one time, theoretically improbable but psychologically quite possible.

You know how you imagine being with a loved one who is a thousand miles away? Well, bam! You are there. That is the reality of the psyche. Marie-Louise von Franz learned that lesson from Jung himself. In 1933, at the age of eighteen, she attended a lecture by the fifty-eight-year-old Jung. In his talk, Jung referred to a schizophrenic woman he had treated who "lived on the moon."

> The young Marie-Louise asked timorously if he meant that it was "as if" she lived on the moon. Jung replied, "No, not 'as if,' she *did* live on the moon."[44]

That's just by-the-by. I often reread such things when I don't know what to do next, hoping that something will get constellated and I can start rolling again. But this day it did nothing to change my mood. What is the opposite of a rolling blade? *Answer:* The big sleep. I could think of nothing better to do than to take the matter to Adam, so off I went.

I found him in a pensive mood. A young nurse bustled in and out, doing her duty. Pretty enough, but not a patch on Pam. When I caught her eye there was no sparkle, indeed hardly any light at all. Just

---

[44] Von Franz, *Animus and Anima in Fairy Tales* p. 6. This was the beginning of an extraordinary relationship between the two. The next year she began to work with Jung, first in analysis and then as his assistant in translating arcane alchemical texts from Latin and Greek. After Jung's death in 1961, she continued to make a name for herself as writer and analyst until she passed away in 1998.

as well. My life was complicated enough already.

I pulled up a chair.

"How are things?" I said lightly.

Adam brushed the question aside and spoke his mind, which was somewhere else, reliving the past. Old people often do that; it's as normal as forgetting yesterday. I was on the tip of that myself, so I didn't mind indulging Adam.

"What is there about love," he said, "that makes us so stupid? I have always enjoyed the intoxication, but I've never become used to the hangover."

I settled back and listened.

"A long time ago," said Adam, "when you were but a tad in the swim of life, I became involved with a woman who pushed all my buttons, and I hers. We didn't do that deliberately, it just happened. Of course at first we were head over heels. She was so completely other that I was besotted.

"Gina was second generation Italian: fiery, passionate, effusive. She expressed herself in exclamation marks. I was fascinated by her easy extraversion, her openness to anything new, her off-the-wall perspective on life. She appreciated my thoughtful manner and introverted attention to detail. She took me out of myself, a breath of fresh air, and I introduced her to a philosophical way of thinking. But what attracted us to each other in the beginning drove us apart in the end. We were forever at odds, you see."

"In what ways?" I asked, ever the pretend Dummling.

"Well," said Adam, "there was her cavalier attitude toward time. She had little sense of the passing of it, whereas I measured everything I did in terms of so many hours, minutes or days. When we'd go out, she was never ready, always late. That was life to her: what's a few minutes here or there, an hour or two? 'Loosen up,' she'd say, as if her behavior were a private matter that didn't affect others, especially me, who often as not was the one kept waiting. And she never apologized because from her point of view the problem was mine! And you know what? Perhaps it was, for in those days I was pathologically punctual, as if the world turning depended on me being on time. I should have left that to the Swiss, it's their vocation.

"In any case, our timetables were seldom in sync. I was an early-to-bed, early riser; you can get so much more done in the quiet morning hours, don't you find? Gina liked to stay up late watching reruns of sit-coms that bored me silly, like *Sex in the City*. I'd be asleep by the time she switched off. We just kept missing each other."

"And what else?" I prompted.

I did like listening to Adam. There's Big Brothers, where you mentor a kid. Well, how about starting an organization called Sons of Guns, where all you'd do is listen to seniors and monitor their meds? I could cry thinking of what is forever lost when people pass away without leaving their personal stories behind. I can't say for sure, but maybe Adam felt something similar, and that was why he was telling me these things.

"I was neat and tidy," he said, "well organized, a place for everything, everything in its place. I made my bed getting out of it, and I wouldn't leave dishes in the sink if you paid me. Gina lived in a dithery, chaotic mess. She was given to acting spontaneously. That's quite a charming trait in the abstract, but very annoying if you prefer order and routine. Know what I mean?"

I nodded. I was taking this down in shorthand.

"Gina would disappear for a few days, sometimes weeks—off she'd go on a new adventure, with not a hint to me. I'd cool my heels with worry and barely resist reporting her as a Missing Person. She was what you'd call a free spirit, and in those years I was not. I was timorous and I didn't like surprises. I was afraid of my shadow and so the unknown made me anxious.

"We also had different ideas on how to spend our leisure time. She favored classical music, ballet and experimental dance. I preferred jazz, pubs and pool halls."

I could sure identify with that.

Adam lay back. His eyes were closed, but his eyelids flickered, as if something was going on behind them.

"Anything else?" I prompted.

"Well, there was what I think of as her health complex."

"Her health complex?!"

"Yes," said Adam. "Gina had an unshakable faith in homeopathic remedies: acupuncture, chiropractic, colonics, hair analysis, chelation therapy, Shiatsu, Reiki, cranial massage and the like. Don't misunderstand me. I don't mean to make fun of her, because I actually learned a lot from Gina about alternative medicine. I even tried some things myself, though I drew the line at fingernail analysis. Maybe I wasn't enough of a believer, but none of it had any effect on me."

"And what else?" I prodded.

Adam sighed. "She'd snipe."

"Snipe?!"

"Well, she'd say things that cut me to the quick. She criticized the length of my hair, the clothes I wore, the food I ate, the books I read, the things I said. She held a grudge longer than the Mississippi, forever bringing up past comments of mine that had been hurtful to her, things I'd long forgotten. And my penchant for whiskey drove her up the wall. Of course I didn't fault her for that. Drinking can shorten one's life, we all know that. And spirit in a bottle, as Jung said, is no substitute for the real thing.[45] Anyway, it's one of my pleasures and I'm not about to give it up. So maybe I won't live to be a hundred, as if that were something to look forward to or be proud of."

I said, "And why ever not?"

"Look at me," grunted Adam. "All these pills and tubes, and all they feed me is mush—baby food that without salt tastes like sawdust, and when I ask for salt they say it's bad for me! 'Bad?' I say, politely as I can. 'Do you know how old I am? Do you actually think a pinch of salt will kill me? What do you know about bad? Bad is when you won't give me what I want; that's bad, and telling me what's good for me is even worse!' They laugh, the doctors, as if I'm a sit-down comic. But not Pam; no sir, that young lady has been a godsend; she

---

[45] It is now well known that Jung was unwittingly instrumental in the founding of Alcoholics Anonymous. Roland H., co-founder—with Bill W.—of AA, had been a patient of Jung's in the 1930s. The relevant correspondence appears as an appendix in Jan Bauer, *Alcoholism and Women: The Background and the Psychology.*

sneaks me little treats from the kitchen. She always has a happy face and seems to enjoy my stories. She even slips me a mickey of the hard stuff now and then."

"She's a real sweetheart," I agreed.

"I can't walk," said Adam, "and I can hardly wash or dress myself. Life at my age is a damned nuisance if you ask me. I'm ready to go anytime."

"Say hello to Sunny for me," I said cheerfully.

I empathized, that's what I do for a living. But I did not go overboard; I did not identify with Adam's maudlin mood—an aspect of the "poor me" syndrome which I knew inside out from times when I was in the dumps myself. Of course he did have more reason than me to complain. He was, after all, closer to the Golden Gates.

Anyway, I think he wasn't listening. He went on about his long-lost love, his Gina. To tell the truth I felt he was well quit of her.

"She had opinions on just about everything," said Adam. "When I questioned them she'd feel offended and say I didn't respect her. Then I'd become defensive, apologize, explain—anything to make things right. I just wanted to be loved for who I was. She wanted me to be someone else, though I was never sure who."

Well, I know a mother complex when I hear it. But I didn't say that out loud because I was Adam's friend, not his analyst.

"Couldn't you talk things over?" I asked.

"Sure! We often did, but that only made matters worse. We'd start out calm as you please, very rational and civilized, but soon enough I'd accidentally push one of her buttons and her inner man would put the boots to me. That roused my inner woman of course, and then we—Gina and I—took a back seat. They would shout and spit at each other, throw eggs, tomatoes, pots and pans, chairs, lamps, anything that wasn't tied down, and we wouldn't know what hit us till the next morning. We'd wake up making love and wonder why the house was in such a mess."

I could hardly cry for laughing, or laugh for crying. For a few minutes I was all stopped up.

"Get the picture?" said Adam.

"Yes," I said. "I too have been in that ballpark. Jung said it like this"—and I quoted from memory:

When animus and anima meet, the animus draws his sword of power and the anima ejects her poison of illusion and seduction.[46]

"That's just how it was," nodded Adam. "We weren't psychologically naive, but we were typologically very different. Like I said, that drew us together at first but tore us apart at last. And perhaps her inner partner was jealous of me, and mine of her. That happens, you know; they can get you from inside, needling: 'He's not good enough for you,' and 'She's not in your class.' Insidious, poisonous, if you don't talk back and state how you feel.

"Anyway, our loving times became few and far between. Animosity was always in the air. One time I even tried to spank her! She belted me right back. That was the beginning of the end.

"But you know, in spite of all that went wrong between us, I was finally able to accept Gina as she was. So I was really hurt when she called it quits. 'It's just not a good fit,' she said. 'You're still waters and what I need at this time in my life are rapids, white caps, rolling waves.' And then she was gone. Two years getting under each other's skin, then toodle-oo. I heard that she took up with a crane operator, a real he-man."

I groped for what to say.

"Well . . . you learned something about relationships . . . what worked for you, what didn't."

"That is true," sighed Adam, "and maybe she did too. In retrospect I think she was right to pull the plug. It freed us both for a better life. You know what Jung says about the good and the better."

I restrained myself from reminding Adam that together we had written a book based on that premise. I mean, why would I make him feel guilty because of something I remember that he didn't? Well, I just plain wouldn't. We all have selective memories, that's the truth.

Anyway, Adam hadn't finished.

---

[46] *Aion*, CW 9ii, par. 30.

"It's not that what we had was all that good, understand; clearly it wasn't, but it hit me hard. For a long time after I couldn't recall the rocky ride, only the loving, the taste and smell of her. But do you know what I missed most of all? Even more than making love? Two things. First, shopping together! I wept recalling the two of us waltzing happily arm in arm through the market, picking up rare herbs and spices, exotic fruits, vegetables, olive oil, home-cooked pastries, sampling cheese and sausage rolls, whatever was offered, all that. And then, Scrabble! She was a sharp player, I hardly ever beat her."

He lay back and closed his eyes. "Sometimes," he said, "I have the memory of an elephant. At other times I draw a blank. I think my mind is going. Just where to I don't know, but I hope it takes me too, and I wouldn't mind if it's sooner rather than later."

I was quiet, digesting Adam. He was a good meal, always was, no doubt about that. But I never knew how much of what he said to take seriously. I was pretty sure he wasn't ready to let go of life, and I received his occasional remarks to the contrary as so much blather. Nevertheless, I thought of advising him to keep his end-of-life comments to himself, for fear the shrinks in charge might put him on suicide watch. And then, of course, no more twinkling sparkles or mickeys from Nurse Pam.

Adam suddenly sat up.

"Dear boy, I've been babbling again," he said. "You didn't come to hear all that. Come closer, laddie. What can I do for you?"

Just about everything, I thought. I felt tears welling up. That's the power of projection.

"Are you jumping through hoops?" he asked. "Your eyes are watering. Is that a genetic condition or are you hopelessly sentimental? Or what else? Don't sweat it, laddie. Hoops! They're just more ball wannabes. Give it to me straight and soon, I could go any minute."

It only took a few words.

"I'm lonely and I've run dry," I said. "I miss Pam."

"That makes two of us," Adam said. "Those flashing eyes make me weak in the knees. But from where I sit, you're in a better position to put the ball in the hoop."

"It's no game to me," I said seriously.

Adam grunted, "Come now, what do you know about her?"

"Very little," I admitted.

"Me too!" cried Adam, "and that's the most fertile ground for love. Need I remind you? The less we know about someone, the easier it is to project. We fill the void with ourselves. We create imaginary relationships that have little or nothing to do with the people we think we're relating to."

"So, what am I to do?" I felt so helpless.

My inner Adam said: "How would I know?"

The real Adam was not so reluctant to give advice.

"Believe in what you feel," he said. "Act on it if you must, but don't take it to heart. Down the road you could be whistling Dixie. Take your time, enjoy the dance, but don't identify with it. Tend your fire and relish the sparks, but take care not to get burned."

Thus saith the Master.

"And what else?" Boy, I do like that question.

"Talk to yourself," said Adam. "Be patient. Don't forget that just as nature corrects herself in the outside world, the psyche is self-regulating. Keep track of your dreams and mull them over. And loneliness? I know it well; feels like you've been abandoned, right? But remember what Jung said—abandonment is a necessary condition of becoming conscious.[47] It's a small price to pay for individuation."

His sparkleNot nurse came in then and said it was time for his nap. I leaned over and brushed my lips on his forehead. Adam smiled and closed his eyes.

---

[47] "The Psychology of the Child Archetype," *The Archetypes and the Collective Unconscious,* CW 9i, pars. 287ff.

8
Ballin' with Rachel

Back home I got to thinking about solitude, being alone, loneliness, abandonment, all that. I paced up and down, feeling bereft. I watched the six o'clock news on TV. It was utterly depressing: wars, suicide bombings, train wrecks, floods, famine, forest fires, child porn, SARS, AIDS, West Nile and so on; terrible things happening all over the world—while here was I, safe as houses, with virtually everything I wanted. Thousands died in the few minutes I spent wondering what shirt to wear or what to put in my next home-made soup.

I felt ashamed. I began to blubber. I was a no-good narcissist. I thought of Kafka's description of himself as "an incapable, ignorant person fit only to crouch in a kennel, to leap out when food is offered and to leap back when he has swallowed it."[48] That was me!

So much for what we call negative inflation. I told myself to stop it. "Stop it!" I said out loud to me. "You are not just that, and you are not without resources!"

Indeed, I had books and notes from other times when I felt like this. I had my active imaginations. I had Jung. And, of course, I had Rachel—thank the Great Unknown for Rachel.

I called her up now with a ditty written by two of the great songwriters of the twentieth century, Jerome Kern and Dorothy Fields. I powered up my Macintosh iTunes program and listened to ol' blue eyes sing "The Way You Look Tonight":

> *Yes, you're lovely, with your smile so warm,*
> *and your cheeks so soft,*
> *there is nothing for me but to love you,*
> *and the way you look tonight.*
> *And that laugh that wrinkles your nose,*
> *touches my foolish heart.*

---

[48] *The Diaries of Franz Kafka*, 1910-1913, p. 308.

Of course, I would like to have sung those lyrics to Nurse Pam, but I didn't dare to. She might think that after all I *was* in love with her, even without going to bed together. And maybe I was, but that was still up for grabs. (Anyway, my Zurich analyst, rest his soul, told me to be very, very careful not to confuse my inner woman with an outer love-interest.)

However, I couldn't hold anything back from Rachel. She did indeed have a warm smile, and cheeks so very soft. Bottom line: between Rachel and me, there could only be full disclosure. She was after all my inner *anam cara,* the soul friend I could not do without. I might have fantasies of other lovelies, even real relationships with them, but not in my wildest dreams would I ever consider hiding anything from Rachel. I should say too that she has many guises, from a swanky Fifth Avenue hostess to a bawdy-house Madame to a Mother Theresa look-alike.[49]

Recall Sleeping Beauty's wicked stepmother asking, "Mirror, mirror, on the wall, who's most beautiful of all?"

Thinking of myself as the mirror, my answer could only be Rachel. In my bevy of lovelies, Rachel is loveliest of all. She is the captain and admiral of lovelies, the doyenne even. She was instrumental in bringing me to my knees so many years ago, painful at the time, but certainly to my benefit. Since then she has often won my heart by breaking it. This is a dichotomy that I don't fully understand but have become used to.

And suddenly there she was.

She had opted to wear her trailer-trash garb: sloppy no-name sandals, low-slung tight-fitting jeans with a good six inches of belly between them and a skimpy tank top. She had silver hoops in her ears, a gold ring in her nose and a pearl in her navel. Her hair was topsy-turvy, as if she'd been sleeping. Which I suppose she had been. I mean, what else would she be doing when she wasn't with me?

Well, whatever she wears, however she looks, I think of Rachel as

---

[49] I get along with most of her personas, but I recently drew the line at her interest in whips. "No thanks," I said. "No problem," she replied. From that I learned, yet again, that I didn't have to cater to her every whim.

my *soror mystica,* generic moniker for the anonymous lovelies who toiled side by side with medieval alchemists as they sweated to transform lead into gold, not knowing that it was their own base selves or *prima materia* (= turd = shadow) that they were working on.

"What time is it?" Rachel yawned, stretching her limbs.

"Time for a little heart to heart," I said.

Oh! she was so beautiful, I was breathless. She was Botticelli's Venus rising out of a foaming sea on a half-shell. Virtually every time she appears, I fall in love anew. I felt a surge of lust. When Rachel manifests like this—as she does two or three times a year—I have to remind myself that traditionally incest is allowed only between kings and queens.[50] For mere mortals it is taboo, a serious no-no. And thus we are obliged to hold a certain amount of tension between what we want and what we are morally or ethically permitted to act out.

Personally, I reckon tension is good for the soul. Just think of what Pam and I were holding. The suppressed longing between us could explode. Theoretically it's possible. $E = mc^2$. If you don't have a release for your energy it could build up inside until poof!—a burst of flame and you're toast. Okay, okay, at least we might blow the lid off a jar of peanut butter.

Well, I hadn't summoned Rachel to hear me preach. I wanted a proper dialogue.

"Rachel," I said. "I've been reading the British psychiatrist Anthony Storr's book, *Solitude.* He believes that the value in being alone is not sufficiently appreciated."

"Good for him," she said. "I'm alone most of the time and I have no complaints. But sure, a lot of people might feel lonely when

---

[50] Although Rachel and I weren't blood relatives, we were psychic intimates, which seems to me to be equivalent. However, I should say that in spite of my personal reserve, dreams of fecundating one's inner woman—or a woman receiving the seed of her inner man—are not uncommon. Indeed, they often lead to the birth of a "divine child," which according to Jung represents "the strongest, the most ineluctable urge in every being, namely the urge to realize [one's wholeness]." ("The Psychology of the Child Archetype," *The Archetypes and the Collective Unconscious,* CW 9i, par. 289) More on this later.

they're alone. Do you think that could be typological? I mean, intro-
verts are generally okay being on their own, but extraverts crave
company, right?"

"Yes, more or less," I agreed, "but that's not the whole story."

I was thinking of what I had written on typology in my other
books and feeling disinclined to repeat it in this one.[51] Sure, there are
some other things here that are repeats, but hey, psychological development is not linear but spiralic—you come back again and again to
see yourself from a different perspective.

"Never mind," said Rachel. She plopped herself in my lap and gave
me a big hug.

Well, I can tell you it feels pretty wonderful to have an inner
woman wrap her arms around you, especially when she looks to be
about forty years younger than yourself.

I pulled myself together.

"Okay, now listen to what Storr says":

Love and friendship are, of course, an important part of what makes life
worthwhile. But they are not the only source of happiness. . . .

. . . Many ordinary interests, and the majority of creative pursuits involving real originality, continue without involving relationships. It
seems to me that what goes on in the human being when he is by himself
is as important as what happens in his interactions with other people. . . .
Two opposing drives operate throughout life: the drive for companionship, love, and everything else which brings us close to our fellow men;
and the drive toward being independent, separate, and autonomous.[52]

"That sure sounds Jungian," remarked Rachel.

"Doesn't it just," I said. "Storr points out that most contemporary
schools of psychology—and particularly developmentalists—put un-
due emphasis on the importance of relationships, while underplaying,
or even ignoring, the benefits in being alone. He challenges the widely
held view that success in intimate relationships is the only key to

---

[51] See my *Personality Types;* also *Jungian Psychology Unplugged: My Life As an
Elephant,* pp. 10ff.

[52] *Solitude,* pp. xiiif.

happiness and psychological health, and points out that in fact the capacity to be alone is crucial if the brain is to function at its best.

"Listen to this":

> Human beings easily become alienated from their own deepest needs and feelings. Learning, thinking, innovation, and maintaining contact with one's own inner world are all facilitated by solitude.[53]

"I like that!" said Rachel. "So where do we go from here?"

"Well, back to Jung of course. As it happens, there is not a single entry on 'solitude' in the index to his Collected Works. *But,* under 'loneliness' there is quite a lot. Of course not all the references are relevant to our current discussion.

"Let's start with this, the down side":

> Every step toward greater consciousness is a kind of Promethean guilt: through knowledge, the gods are as it were robbed of their fire; that is, something that was the property of the unconscious powers is torn out of its natural context and subordinated to the whims of the conscious mind. The man who has usurped the new knowledge suffers, however, a trans-formation or enlargement of consciousness, which no longer resembles that of his fellow men. He has raised himself above the human level of his age . . . but in so doing has alienated himself from humanity. The pain of this loneliness is the vengeance of the gods, for never again can he return to mankind. He is, as the myth says, chained to the lonely cliffs of the Caucasus, forsaken of God and man.[54]

Rachel sniffed.

"Isn't that rather too strong, 'forsaken of God and man'?"

"I don't think so," I said. "That's what it feels like when you break away from the pack, when you stop caring what others will say or think and who they want you to be. I've been there and at first it's lonely, there's no other word for it."

Rachel mused.

---

[53] Ibid., p. 28.

[54] "The Persona as a Segment of the Collective Psyche," *Two Essays On Analytical Psychology,* CW 7, par. 243n.

"I shall have to trust you on that. It was before I knew you."

"Yes, before you were born even."

Sigh, that long ago? How time does pass. My head swam.

I opened another book. "I also found these two passages, where Jung refers to the divine child image in dreams as a harbinger of a new attitude, and to the significance of the child motif in general":

> Higher consciousness, or knowledge going beyond our present-day consciousness, is equivalent to being *all alone in the world.* This loneliness expresses the conflict between the bearer or symbol of higher consciousness and his surroundings.[55]

> The "child" is all that is abandoned and exposed and at the same time divinely powerful; the insignificant, dubious beginning, and the triumphal end. The "eternal child" in man is an indescribable experience, an incongruity, a handicap, and a divine prerogative; an imponderable that determines the ultimate worth or worthlessness of a personality.[56]

Rachel mused again.

"Isn't it true that whether a child image in a dream is to be taken as divine or not is a matter of debate among Jungians?"

I was ready for that.

"Indeed. The child image may refer to the dreamer's own self in early life, or a childish attitude. It all depends on the context—what is happening in the dreamer's life at the time of the dream, and where he or she is in terms of psychological development. Personally, I think an important clue is the rapid growth of the child—from birth to walking and talking in an unrealistically short length of time. That's divine.[57]

---

[55] "The Psychology of the Child Archetype," *The Archetypes and the Collective Unconscious,* CW 9i, par. 288. I am not too happy with the expression "higher" consciousness, which implies a degree of superiority. I think "enlarged" would be a better translation.

[56] Ibid., par. 300.

[57] Edward F. Edinger agrees: "To be 'divine' the child image must have something unusual or out of the ordinary about it. So if you have a dream of a child that is just born and can speak, for instance, that's the divine child." *(The Sacred Psyche: A Psychological Approach to the Psalms,* p. 40)

"When that is an aspect of the dream image, I tend to see the child as Jung does—pointing toward new life for the dreamer, a new perspective. And then you look at the child's gender and try to relate *that* to the dreamer's potential in terms of the masculine and the feminine and how these energies are played out in the person's life. All in all, it can get pretty complicated.

"And then I found these":

[A man's egoism] is his strongest and healthiest power; it is . . . a true will of God, which sometimes drives him into complete isolation. However wretched this state may be, it also stands him in good stead, for in this way alone can he get to know himself and learn what an invaluable treasure is the love of his fellow beings. It is, moreover, only in the state of complete abandonment and loneliness that we experience the helpful powers of our own natures.[58]

Since, as a rule, every concept and every point of view handed down from the past proves futile, we must first tread with the patient the path of his illness—the path of his mistake that sharpens his conflicts and increases his loneliness till it becomes unbearable—hoping that from the psychic depths which cast up the powers of destruction the rescuing forces will also come.[59]

"Loneliness here," said Rachel, "really means solitude, right?"

"Yes," I agreed.

I continued to rummage in Jung's Collected Works. His essays are so seductive, engrossing, stimulating. Sometimes I take a volume, sit it on its spine and let it fall open where it will. Then I soak up what is written, invariably timely in terms of what I need to hear. Or you might start by looking up what he wrote on mothers or dwarfs or fish, say, and one thing leads to another. After twenty-four hours you rub your eyes and see that you haven't got past alchemy. Which as it happened I was now into up to my knees.

"Rachel! Here's a gem:

---

[58] "Psychotherapists or the Clergy," *Psychology and Religion,* CW 11, par. 525.
[59] Ibid., par. 532.

Alchemists were, in fact, decided solitaries; each had his say in his own way. They rarely had pupils, and of direct tradition there seems to have been very little, nor is there much evidence of secret societies or the like. Each worked in the laboratory for himself and suffered from loneliness.[60]

—and speaking of someone who has left the comfortable containment of a religious belief, Jung writes":

You are alone and you are confronted with all the demons of hell. That is what people don't know. Then they say you have an anxiety neurosis, nocturnal fears, compulsions—I don't know what. Your soul has become lonely; it is *extra ecclesiam* [outside the Church] and in a state of no-salvation. And people don't know it. They think your condition is pathological. . . . But it is neurotic talk when one says this is a neurosis. As a matter of fact it is something quite different: it is the terrific fear of loneliness. . . . You can be a member of a society with a thousand members, and you are still alone. That thing in you which should live is alone; nobody touches it, nobody knows it, you yourself don't know it; but it keeps on stirring, it disturbs you, it makes you restless, and it gives you no peace.[61]

"Wow!" said Rachel.

She had meanwhile done some rummaging of her own.

"Here, listen to this":

The antidote to the fear of losing the world is to let go of it. The antidote for loneliness is to embrace loneliness. As in homeopathy, the wound is healed by swallowing a bit of the toxin itself.

The paradox of relationship, which we in the Western world seem to hold as the cure for all ills, is that the more one embraces one's separateness, the more one can live with oneself, the better relationship will be.[62]

"So true, so true," I said.

Rachel asked: "When is loneliness *not* a swampland? I mean, as opposed to the positive experience of solitude?"

---

[60] "Religious Ideas in Alchemy," *Psychology and Alchemy*, CW 12, par. 422.

[61] "The Symbolic Life," *The Symbolic Life*, CW 18, par. 632.

[62] James Hollis, *Swamplands of the Soul: New Life in Dismal Places*, p. 65.

A good question. I thought about it.

"Well, it's sure no fun to be alone when you long for someone to be intimate with. But if being on your own is a fact of your life, I think you're obliged to make the best of it. Turn your fear of loneliness into an appreciation of solitude. Think of it: you're a grown-up! You can do what you want! You don't need anyone's permission! In your aloneness you might even create something.

"And meanwhile, you can keep an eagle eye out for someone to be with you on your journey. It's wonderful to have someone to love, and love you back, but don't give up the ghost and think you're nobody without a partner. And don't equate loneliness with being alone."

Rachel clapped. "Oh, you say it so well!"

What a sweetheart, always on my side; well, more or less.

And then suddenly I'd had enough.

Still, I thought it proper to give the last word to Jung himself. In his autobiography he confesses that as a child he had felt himself to be alone, and at the age of 86, still did. Here is how he put it:

> Loneliness does not come from having no people about one, but from being unable to communicate the things that seem important to oneself, or from holding certain views which others find inadmissible. The loneliness began with the experiences of my early dreams, and reached its climax at the time I was working on the unconscious. If a man knows more than others, he becomes lonely. But loneliness is not necessarily inimical to companionship, for no one is more sensitive to companionship than the lonely man, and companionship thrives only when each individual remembers his individuality and does not identify himself with others.[63]

I embraced Rachel, tucked her in, and turned out the light.

That night I took myself off to Ben Wick's, a pub in the downtown core managed by the always-genial Robert. There I was entertained by Whisky Jack, a quartet of joyful musicians led by Banjo-Devil Duncan, one of my snooker-playing buddies who toured for years with Stompin' Tom Connors before becoming a real-estate

---

[63] *Memories, Dreams, Reflections*, p. 356.

agent. His sidekicks Arlene and Bob and Howard did not disappoint. I sang along with gusto to "Ghost Riders in the Sky," as I usually do.

It was a fine gig and I sparkled with a sexy granny who in 1999 was dubbed "Champion Knitter of the Niagara Peninsula." She was a lovely but didn't know it. She gave me a polka dot scarf for the gargoyle who with child on knee squats watch beside my front steps. He is a threshold god, apotropaically protecting my house from evil. His name is Arnold.

I went to bed fragmented, but content.

Arnold and child

9
The Razor's Edge

"I tend to be attracted to intuitives," I was saying. "They have a 'something' that I don't, which is a keen sense of possibilities and what's going on in other people. Jung calls it the function that mediates perceptions in an unconscious way—a kind of instinctive apprehension, quite irrational."[64]

Pam and I were walking hand-in-hand, cruising along the lake front. It was a warm July evening and music was everywhere. A Mexican festival had just begun, with a side-bar of Indian dance. There were lots of people in colorful costumes, acrobats doing back-flips, shell-game con artists, portrait painters, magicians pulling scarves out of hats and coins from ears and noses, and some tricksters promising to turn lead into gold—wannabe alchemists.

I was toting a knapsack with a few books in it, just in case.

"And I have a soft spot for sensation types," smiled Pam. "I envy the way they move in the world, their ease with time and space and, oh, just things as they are! When I was a student I wasn't worried about the exams. But I was terrified I wouldn't get to the right place at the right time. That would keep me awake the whole night before!"

"Sensation and intuition are opposites," I said. "Both are functions of perception, but sensation is conscious and intuition is not.[65]

"Think about the difference between intuitives and sensation types when they enter an empty house. The sensation function sees just what is right there at that moment: the bare walls, shabby windows, dirty floors, the creaky porch. Intuition sees the same mundane scene, but transformed in the mind's eye according to what could be done with it—walls painted in soft pastels, pictures in place, floors sanded and polished, clean windows and elegant curtains, even where the furniture will go."

---

[64] "Definitions," *Psychological Types,* CW 6, pars. 770ff.
[65] Ibid., pars. 792ff

"Then you'd better take me along when you go shopping for a house," laughed Pam.

"Love to," I smiled, "and of course the reverse is true too. If you were buying a house you might be spellbound by the possibilities. You'd see the place furnished and completely redecorated, everything hunky-dory, no problems at all. I'd notice damp seeping into the basement, the state of the plumbing and the roof, the number of electrical plugs, the distance to the nearest school and shops, all that and a whole lot more."

"So you'd be lost without me," she said, "and I'd be lost without you, is that it?" She hugged me.

"I guess, at least if we were buying houses."

Glowing with Pam I felt pretty good.

We stopped at a roadside vendor and bought ice-cream cones smothered in nuts and chocolate. We sat on a bench and tried to keep one lick ahead of the drips.

"What do you want from a woman?" asked Pam. "What would suit you best?"

They were fair questions and I gave them serious thought. What would suit me best? Well, I wouldn't mind being rocked in a cradle, my mother's voice soothing me to sleep. And I'd like to be responsible for nothing. But I couldn't get away with that because I'm no longer psychologically naive and I have irons in the fire that need my attention. I'd certainly have nightmares if I tried to opt out. So, given all that, realistically, what do I want from a woman?

I said to Pam: "I want to feel loved. I want to be close to a woman, physically and emotionally, but psychologically separate. I don't want to live in her pocket and I don't want her in mine. I'm not looking for a wife or a roommate. I like having my own space. I want a lover and a soul friend—as opposed to a soul mate. I would like someone to hold hands with when we're out on the town. I want to think of her as my sweetheart. I wouldn't mind if she had other men friends, but I'd rather she didn't sleep with them."

That was as honest as I could be out loud, and true enough to what I knew about myself.

"So, what's the difference," asked Pam, "between a soul mate, a soul friend, and a sweetheart?"

I'd actually thought about that. "The notion of a soul mate," I said, "carries with it the archetypal expectation of wholeness—like, together the two of you are one, complete. An *anam cara* or soul friend is someone you acknowledge to be quite other and appreciate as such. A sweetheart is simply a romantic concept."

"Mr. Formality, meet Miss Concept!" whooped Pam. "And if they have a child?"

"It depends on how well they get along," I shrugged. "Misconception . . . immaculate conception . . ."

Pam laughed. "There, you're as goofy as I am when you let yourself go! And what kind of man would rather have a sweetheart than a soul mate?"

Now this was a question that had never occurred to me, but I had a stab at answering.

"Perhaps," I said, "one who has had enough experience with relationships to be aware of the role played by projection. You see, the idea of a soul mate implies that we're incomplete without a lost other half.[66] And maybe we are, but I don't think we'll find our completion with someone in the outside world. It's our contrasexual inner other, anima or animus, who is more properly the object of our search. Without that intrapsychic relationship you easily get seduced by the ideal of togetherness, which lets you off the hook of self-understanding. Granted, individuation isn't possible without the mirroring that goes with relationship, but to my mind it's not compatible with the stickiness of togetherness."

Pam nodded.

"So," I continued, "all in all, I'd go for a sweetheart who feels the same way, And then, you see, I'd automatically have a soul friend, and possibly even a lover . . ."

---

[66] In Plato's *Symposium* (14-16; 189A-193E), for instance, Aristophanes pictures humans as originally whole but arrogant. As punishment Zeus cut them in half, and that is why, it is said, we forever seek to replace that lost other.

"And what if she were married?" teased Pam.

"Not my business," I lied.

"Okay," she nodded. "Then where does a loverNot fit in? Is she just a spare tire, someone to be goofy with when you're not romancing the latest lovely to catch your fancy?"

I stopped walking and faced her. "Pam, you silly, a loverNot is at the top of the food chain! She is soul mate, soul friend and sweetheart all in one. A single loverNot, all by herself, is a trinity of anima figures. She gives substance to a man's inner harem."

I held her close. Passersby smiled.

"Thank you." She touched my cheek, a tender gesture that whisked me to the stars.[67] I hovered there for a few seconds.

Back on earth, I said: "When you know what you have to do—what consciously feels right—and then do it, the next question is how much you have to keep to yourself. Can you stand the tension between who others think you are and who you know yourself to be? You think of your loved ones and how some of them would be hurt if they knew what you and your shadow were up to. Is that a reason to backtrack, conform with expectations? I don't think so."

"What if you later regret what you did?" asked Pam.

"You can't turn back time," I said. "If it doesn't work, move on to your next experiment in creative living."

I stopped talking. I handed Pam the earphones to my portable player and put on a CD of the 60's pop group Buffalo Springfield, *Last Time Around*. I fast-forwarded to "Kind Woman." Don't ask me why. Sometimes a cigar is just a cigar.

> *Kind woman,*
> *Won't you love me tonight.*
> *I look in your eyes*
> *Kind woman,*
> *Don't leave me lonely tonight.*

---

[67] "Touch is such an immediate sense. . . . [It] offers the deepest clue to the mystery of encounter, awakening, and belonging. It is the secret, affective content of every connection and association The energy, warmth and invitation of touch come ultimately from the divine." (O'Donohue, *Anam Cara*, p. 75)

Pam listened to the end of the song. She handed the earphones back to me. "So romantic," she sighed. "I can almost believe in it." "Me too," I said.

We walked along, hand in hand. With weather this fine, I imagined we might go on forever. But alas, my calves were starting to hurt. This was not new. It was due to poor circulation in my lower limbs; they just didn't get enough oxygen. After I walked for ten minutes or so, I had to stop and let the blood flow catch up.[68]

I guided Pam to a bench and we rested. She tucked her head into the crook between my chin and shoulder. I loved her in silence. So much to say. So much not to. I dozed and thought back to a dream I had soon after returning to Toronto from my years training in Zurich:

I was in a university lecture theater, giving a talk to a class of first year psychology students. I had drawn diagrams on the blackboard.

"And that's what life's all about," I concluded jauntily, tossing the chalk in the air. I had my eye on a young co-ed seated about half-way back. She was button-cute and smiling.

A boy in the first row stood up. He was maybe nineteen.

"Isn't it true," he said, "that you left your family?"

He looked around at the others and snickered. The audience murmured.

"I did."

"You abandoned your wife and kids?"

I hung my head. "I did."

"You left them *penniless?"*

"Wait, you don't understand . . . I had no choice . . ."

The young snot took a whip from his waistband and was about to lash me when Jung himself appeared, stage right.

"Stop this!" he shouted. He was old, at least eighty. He stooped and had a cane. He hobbled between me and the students.

---

[68] This condition, known as intermittent claudication, reportedly affects more than a million North Americans over the age of fifty. It is caused by the build-up of plaque in the arteries, impeding the flow of blood. It may be alleviated by a medical procedure called angioplasty, where a probe with a quiescent balloon on the end of it snakes through an artery in your groin, and when it comes to a point of blockage the balloon is inflated to blast the nasty plaque to smithereens. Sometimes it works, as it did for me the first time. Now, I guess I was due for another.

"This man," said Jung, pointing to me, "is human. That is his only crime." He turned to me and said, "Go, leave this place. Do your work and be yourself. Stop feeling guilty for who you are."

I awoke with a start, feeling refreshed.

Pam stirred and stretched. "Where were we?"

I thought back. "Let's see . . . I think we were talking about the difference between lovers and loverNots."

Pam smiled. "Yes," she said. "Well, I shouldn't think you'd have much trouble finding someone to fit your wants or needs, whatever. There are lots of unattached women these days who aren't looking for a man to take care of them. They like having their own space. They lead busy lives and aren't particularly lonely. I know some who wouldn't mind having a man to play ball with. We all need someone to love and be loved by, don't you think?"

"I don't know about others," I said, "but I do. When my partner left me last year I felt homeless, disoriented. I began writing a book called *Fear of Floating*. It went nowhere because I couldn't focus. I floundered. I felt like a ship without an anchor, an aimless ball that might bounce off the face of the earth."

Pam hugged me true.

"But sometimes," I said, "I wonder if maybe only those who have a positive mother complex look for someone to love and be loved by."

"What do you mean?" asked Pam.

"Well, the grown man who as a child had a good experience of his personal mother—if, say, she was receptive and nourishing—would long to be loved the same way. We'd say he had a positive mother complex. He'd tend to seek out women who would accept him as unconditionally as his mom did."

"And if they didn't?" said Pam.

"Then he'd see them as bad mothers because they'd forever frustrate his expectations. Of course this can change if he works on himself and gains some understanding of his complexes and relationship patterns, but on the whole he'd avoid such women, simply because they wouldn't answer his need for affection."

"And if a man had a bad experience of his personal mother?"

"He would likely be suspicious of women," I said, "and especially of those who wanted to take care of him—so-called good mothers—or, conversely, respond very well to a woman who'd give him the kind of loving attention he didn't have in early life. In short, he would either look for the opposite of what he knew, or that would be just too alien for comfort, so he'd become attached to a woman who would give him just as hard a time as his mother did."

I was thinking here of Adam and his tie to Gina, but I didn't say it because I felt it was privileged information.

"Well," asked Pam, "is a negative mother complex worse than a positive one?"

"Worse? Not necessarily."

I could think of so much to say that I was tongue-tied. But after a few minutes I had a go at it.

"Good, bad, better, worse—these are value judgments. A complex in itself is neutral. It's the consequences that can be called good or bad. A complex is just a set of emotions associated with an image or idea. When a complex is constellated, when it becomes active, you're bound to react in a certain way. You literally have no choice, and it's generally quite predictable. And if we don't know our complexes, those close to us sure do.

"For instance: 'Don't mention his sister, it drives him up the wall.' 'Stay away from such-and-such, she just gets upset.' 'He can't think straight when you mention his father.' 'Talk of money makes him crazy.' And so on.

"Well, we all have our hot buttons, some topic or idea that touches us emotionally. You can't have a rational conversation with someone in the grip of a complex. The best you can do is back off and change the subject, or just walk away, there's no shame in that. It's like having to shoot the yellow ball, two points, because you messed up and didn't get position on the black, seven points."

I paused for breath.

Pam was looking at me and smiling.

Holy schemolee! Green eyes, just like a cat! You'd think that me being a sensation type I would have noticed this right off the bat.

Well I hadn't. I turned away for fear of drowning in what I took to be a loving gaze.[69]

"So," I said, when I had recovered my wits, "to kind of answer your question, a positive mother complex can actually have negative consequences. For instance, the world at large, where people are judged by what they do, is not positive mother. I mean you're not accepted simply because you're you. You have to earn your place in the world. This can be quite a shock to someone who grew up being accepted at face value as the greatest. Such men tend to feel at home in an institutional setting—the Church, say, or a large corporation, or the civil service—jobs that simulate positive mother, with generous benefits and pension plans and guaranteed long-term security. Is that good or bad? And who's to say? Of course, one's friends probably have an opinion, but since the effect of a complex is primarily subjective, its character can really only be judged from the inside."

Pam tapped her teeth: "I suppose you don't go looking to fix what feels okay."

"True enough," I said. "There are all kinds of complexes. Mother, father, money and power are only the most well known. And the kind of parental complex you start off with, whether you call it positive or negative, isn't the end of the story. A negative mother complex, for example, can have positive consequences in that it might stimulate a healthy independence or enable one to more easily weather life's misfortunes. It can drive a man out of the childhood nest to sink or swim on the sea of life. For example, a man with a positive father complex might assume that his way through life will be smooth, no trouble finding a job and so on, while a man with a negative father complex is better prepared for the fact that he can't take anything for granted and will have to prove himself.

---

[69] I later came across this description of the difference between gazing and staring: "When you really gaze at something, you bring it inside you. One could write a beautiful spirituality on the holiness of the gaze. The opposite of the gaze is the intrusive stare. When you are stared at, the eye of the Other becomes tyrannical. You have become the object of the Other's stare in a humiliating, invasive, and threatening way." (O'Donohue, *Anam Cara*, pp. 60f.)

"So the effects of complexes are truly a mixed bag. It's how you live them out that counts—what you make of what you got, added to what you picked up along the way. These days it's called the nature vs. nurture issue, and postgraduate students write Ph.D.'s on it."

"How does it work for a woman?" asked Pam. "I mean, how does her experience of her father influence her?"

I frowned. I had no personal experience to draw on, so I could only give a theoretical answer. "It seems to vary," I said cautiously. "Just as a man is apt to marry his mother, so to speak—or her exact opposite—so a woman is programmed to favor a man psychologically like her father, or, again, his opposite."

"I guess that covers all the bases, huh?" said Pam wryly.

I laughed. "Yes, but of course consciousness plays a part. That's what analysis is all about. Your reactions to other people and situations can be curbed, or at least modified, if you're aware of your complexes. For instance, whenever you're defensive or overly sensitive, you're caught in a complex."

"Doesn't analysis get rid of complexes?" asked Pam, as if she didn't know better. Well, that suited me. If I didn't have an interlocutor I'd just be talking to myself and that would be no fun at all.

"No," I said, "by definition that's not possible. Complexes are the building blocks of the psyche, just as atoms and molecules make up tables and chairs. By virtue of existing, you have complexes. The question is whether they're active or not—how and when they get constellated—and how they affect your life. Those are the bread and butter issues in analysis."

"But you don't try to get rid of them?" she pressed.

"Can a leopard lose its spots?" I asked. "Without your complexes, you would not be you. Your personality is the result of your complexes. You don't choose them and you can't get quit of them. The most you can do is understand their effects and work at depotentiating the ones that give you trouble."

Pam gestured. "Depotentiate?"

"It means taking away its power," I said, "loosening its influence. When you get to know your complexes, you have a better understanding of who you are and more control over how that's expressed—what you say and do, and so on. For instance, you have an emotional reaction but you don't have to blurt it out. You can hold back and reflect on it: Just where did *that* come from? What came over me?"

Pam nodded, wonderfully spellbound

"The depotentiation of complexes," I went on, "comes about in the process of becoming conscious of them. It happens over a period of time by asking yourself, over and over again—after, say, a heated exchange, an argument, an angry outburst, that kind of thing—what got into me? who was speaking? what got my goat?"[70]

"What happens if you do nothing about your complexes?" asked Pam. "What if you don't even know you have them?"

I threw up my hands. "What doesn't? Wife beating, child abuse, relationship problems of every kind. That's just the tip of the iceberg. You can read about it every day, in every newspaper, in every country. Rape, murder, suicide, war. You could say that news is what happens when someone is complexed. Well, it's not news to me. Complexes aren't always troublesome, but a lot of them are bombs waiting to go off. Actually, it's pretty well known nowadays that people have complexes. What isn't so well known is that complexes can have us. But that's normal, and Jung says as much."

I pulled from my knapsack Jung's thick book on typology. I thumbed through the yellow post-its and read:

> To have complexes does not necessarily indicate inferiority. It only means that something discordant, unassimilated, and antagonistic exists, perhaps as an obstacle, but also as an incentive to greater effort, and so, perhaps, to new possibilities of achievement.[71]

---

[70] The idiomatic association of complexes and goats is, I think, no accident. The meat of a goat was the original sacrifice to the gods, in hopes of averting catastrophe. Later it was people who were sacrificed—"scapegoats"; they bore the brunt for the emotions people couldn't cope with—guilt, shame and so on. (See Sylvia Brinton Perera, *The Scapegoat Complex: Toward a Mythology of Shadow and Guilt)*

[71] "A Psychological Theory of Types," *Psychological Types,* CW 6, par. 925.

"Complexes work both ways, you see. They can stimulate us to greater consciousness and the better use of our abilities, or they can tie us up in knots. As long as we don't know about them, we're at their mercy."

"Then we're neurotic!" cried Pam.

"Possibly, but not necessarily. Here's what Jung says"—and I dug out another volume:

> The possession of complexes does not in itself signify neurosis . . . and the fact that they are painful is no proof of pathological disturbance. Suffering is not an illness; it is the normal counterpole to happiness. A complex becomes pathological only when we think we have not got it.[72]

She nodded. "The old adage, 'Know Thyself' . . ."

We got up and touched noses. Pam took my hand and we continued our stroll.

"Yes," I agreed, "but the Greeks didn't know the half of it. They knew only of the conscious mind. The vast area of psychic activity we now call the unconscious was not even conceived of in those days. Complexes are by definition more or less unconscious, so they're always liable to boil up. Analysis can take the steam out of them, but some complexes you just learn to live with. It's like they're little devils hiding in the woodwork. One way or another, no matter how conscious you think you are, from time to time they will turn you inside out. For instance, you might work on your feelings about an old lover for years, but still, whenever you run into that person you feel on edge, you're not yourself.

"Likewise, you can analyze every detail of a miserable childhood and still get the jitters when you see your parents. That's the reality of the psyche. Getting to know your complexes doesn't make you invulnerable, but at least it prepares you for what to expect."

Pam nodded. "And what of soul," she asked. "Where or when does soul come into play?"

---

[72] "Psychotherapy and a Philosophy of Life," *The Practice of Psychotherapy,* CW 16, par. 179.

"Always, and in every way," I said. "I think that if you try to nail down soul in so many words, it just slip-slides away . . . I think that soul manifests in what goes on between people, day to day. I think that soul ought not to be thought of as an esoteric concept, but as an appreciation of the matter-of-fact. And hey, if what is going on between you and me is not soul, what is?"

Pam smiled. "Yes, we do experience soul-play and all its wonders when we're together, but the pure and simple acceptance of that as a 'just-so story' is not enough for me. Maybe it has something to do with typology. You are rooted in the here and now, and I am not."

"I am listening," I said.

Pam said: "Just think of all the poets, writers, painters, dancers, sculptors, film-makers, philosophers, theologians, all those who have struggled with their experiences of soul—ineffable as it is—and see what they have created. The attempt to define the mystery of soul often manifests in beautiful creations."

"How true," I agreed, and for awhile we ambled along in silence.

"And what of you?" I asked at length. "What do you want that you don't already have?"

Pam didn't answer right away. She kept hold of my hand but she didn't look at me.

"Sweetheart?" I prompted. "LoverNot? *Anam cara?*"

Pam cast her eyes up, around and about, settling on the newly installed wind turbine close to the waterfront, not so far away from where we were. It's hard to miss: 300 feet high with a propeller wingspan like a 747.[73]

"Everything and nothing," she said finally.

Well, who could fault that. I didn't press for more. Maybe one day she'd write her own book.

---

[73] I was inordinately proud of this local landmark because my daughter-in-law Deb, a head honcho in wind energy circles, was instrumental in making it happen. Of course, I was also mindful of wind as symbolically associated with the divine spirit.

10
The Crystal Ball

Pam and Adam and I were in a huddle on Adam's patio. There was a slight chill in the air, but the sun was out and it felt good to be right where we were. Oh, and Luigi was there too. I'd brought him along for the ride, and also, to be frank, because he had made the sandwiches for our lunch-to-be.

We were then a quaternity of forces, functionally different typologically. To be explicit, I saw us this way:

Adam, an extraverted thinking-sensation type; Pam, extraverted feeling-intuition; myself, introverted thinking-sensation; and Luigi, a typological bowl of soup. I may well be wrong, but that's my call.

There was a small pile of books on a side table. We had finished the *New York Times* weekly crossword—well, most of it—and now were working on a fairy tale, just for the fun of thinking symbolically.[74]

After some good-natured banter we had chosen a favorite of Adam's, "The Crystal Ball."[75] It begins like this:

There was once an enchantress who had three sons who loved each other as brothers, but the old woman did not trust them, and thought they wanted to steal her power from her. So she changed the eldest into an eagle, which was forced to dwell in the rocky mountains, and was often seen flying in great circles in the sky. The second, she changed into a whale, which lived in the deep sea, and all that was seen of it was that it sometimes spouted up a great jet of water in the air. Each of them bore his human form for only two hours daily. The third son, who was afraid she might change him into a raging wild beast—a bear perhaps, or a wolf, went secretly away.

---

[74] A symbol, according to Jung, is the best possible expression for something essentially unknown. (See "Definitions," *Psychological Types,* CW 6, pars. 814ff) Nowadays, symbolic thinking is seen as nonlinear, right-brain oriented, complementary to logical, linear, left-brain thinking.

[75] *Complete Grimm's Fairy Tales,* pp. 798ff.

He had heard that a King's daughter was bewitched, was imprisoned in the Castle of the Golden Sun, and was waiting to be set free. Those, however, who tried to free her risked their lives; three and twenty youths had already died a miserable death, and now only one other might make the attempt, after which no more must come. And as his heart was without fear, he made up his mind to seek out the Castle of the Golden Sun.

"What do you make of the initial situation?" asked Adam.[76]

"Clearly there's a lack of Eros, the positive feminine principle," said Pam. "The enchantress does not love her sons; she is the personification of power."

Adam nodded and pulled out a volume of Jung's Collected Works. He read:

Where love reigns, there is no will to power; and where the will to power is paramount, love is lacking.[77]

"You see," he said, "logically the opposite of love is hate, but psychologically the opposite of love is the will to power."

That was heavy and we were quiet for a few minutes. I think it was clear to each of us that if you loved someone, you would have to relinquish power over them.

"There's a quaternity," I noted, "enchantress and three sons, but no mature masculine, no Logos." I drew a crude sketch:

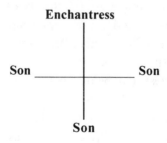

---

[76] I believe he had in mind an instruction by Marie-Louise von Franz to note carefully what is missing at the start of a fairy tale, and whether that lack is corrected, or not, in the end. (See her *Interpretation of Fairy Tales*, pp. 27ff.)

[77] *Two Essays on Analytical Psychology*, CW 7, par. 78.

"We're a quaternity too," Luigi pointed out, "and Pam has enchanted us, like three sons."

"Hold on," objected Pam, "An enchantress is equivalent to a witch, right? A devouring mother? I'd rather be good mother."

Wouldn't we all, I thought, not to mention wishing we'd had one.

I said: "Don't worry, you get redeemed in the end."

Adam asked, "What might that look like in real life, a devouring mother?"

"Well," said Pam, "a woman who wouldn't allow her children to lead their own lives. She'd be intrusive, controlling. Under her influence they might be compelled to act out her unlived life. That's a form of bewitchment."

Adam: "Good, good. And on a collective level?"

"To me," I said, "it suggests a society or civilization in which customs and habits have become rigid, with highly regulated institutions that have no heart for exceptions. Ethics, for instance! You couldn't wiggle your toe at a lovely for fear of breaching some friggin' Code!"

We laughed

"Archetypally," offered Pam (and how I admired the ease with which that word rolled off her tongue), "the situation is controlled by the negative feminine."

"Indeed," I agreed. "That's more or less equivalent to what we'd call an animus-possessed woman. And in terms of masculine psychology it would be a man motivated by power—opinionated, moody, unrelated to his unconscious and therefore dominated by his inner woman; in short, anima-possessed."

"What about the eldest son being changed into an eagle?" asked Luigi.

Adam said: "Symbolically, the eagle is identified with the sun, the idea of male activity and masculine consciousness—Logos, the spiritual principle. Of all birds, the eagle flies the highest. In heraldry, the imperial eagle is a symbol of power, nobility and wisdom. In alchemy it represents the volatile spirit, as opposed to the earthbound lion."

"Which means?" Luigi scratched his head.

I jumped in. "In a man's psychology he would be that spiritual element that is always seeking the light of higher consciousness, the meaning of life. According to Jung this can be one of the positive effects of the mother complex." I plucked a book off the pile and read:

> What in its negative aspect is Don Juanism can appear positively as bold and resolute manliness; ambitious striving after the highest goals; opposition to all stupidity, narrowmindedness, injustice and laziness; willingness to make sacrifices for what is regarded as right, sometimes bordering on heroism; perseverance, inflexibility and toughness of will; a curiosity that does not shrink even from the riddles of the universe; and finally, a revolutionary spirit which strives to put a new face upon the world.[78]

Pam clapped. "How wonderful!"

She looked at me and Morse-coded her appreciation. I blinked back my thanks for everything.

"Of course there's a negative side to the eagle too," I went on. "In Greek mythology there's the legend of Prometheus, whose liver was daily devoured by an eagle and nightly renewed. That was his punishment for giving mankind the fire of the gods, fire representing consciousness."

"The Greeks," added Adam, "regarded the liver as the inmost spring of the deeper emotions. You know the expression 'to eat one's liver,' referring to striving after the unattainable? So psychologically the eagle is also that element in a man that is perhaps too idealistic, too much up in the air. For instance, it's a common characteristic of puers to flap around in great circles getting nowhere—to live in the rarified air of the spirit and neglect the here and now."

"Meanwhile, at the other extreme," said Luigi, "there is the brother who's changed into a whale."

"Yes," said Pam. "Whereas the eagle is master of the sky, the whale is at home in the sea, which symbolically represents the unconscious on account of its vastness and depth."

I said: "The whale is the largest mammal, and as a matter of fact

---

[78] "Psychological Aspects of the Mother Archetype," *The Archetypes and the Collective Unconscious,* CW 9i, par. 165.

it's the first animal mentioned in the Bible by name. (Gen. 1:21) The whale is also often pictured as the container of the hero during his perilous night-sea journey—as in the story of Jonah and the whale, and Pinocchio too."

I thought of the great white whale in Melville's novel *Moby-Dick,* and Edward F. Edinger's psychological interpretation,[79] but I did not mention it for fear it would take us too far afield.

Pam spoke: "In Shakespeare the whale appears as a symbol of lust. Remember, in *All's Well That Ends Well,* the young count 'who is a whale to virginity'?[80] So it's connected with the unconscious and the so-called baser instincts."

Oh! Maybe Pam wrote a paper on it too.

"And yet," said Adam, "it is also crucial to the hero's salvation, as we'll see in the end. You see, neither the eagle nor the whale are negative symbols per se, but here they are in the power of the negative feminine. In a man, the bewitchment of his inner eagle and whale natures would likely manifest as mood swings, sudden or inexplicable ups and downs."

"Think of Franz Kafka," I put out, "a man with a pronounced negative mother complex, who declared that he could be raised to the heights with lightning speed—there's the enthusiasm of creation—or be crushed forever as if by the weight of the seas—a metaphor for depression."[81]

Adam nodded and asked, "In our fairy tale, what might balance these extremes?"

You could hear gears grinding.

Luigi spoke first: "The youngest brother?"

"Exactly!" said Adam, "the Dummling or Stupid Hans we know from other tales. I like to think of this figure as representing an aspect of the individual psyche that has not been coerced or co-opted by collective pressures. We all had it at first, in childhood, and still do,

---

[79] *Melville's Moby-Dick: An American Nekyia.*

[80] Act. 4, scene 3.

[81] See my *Secret Raven: Conflict and Transformation,* p. 111.

though buried under the accretions of daily life—a virgin innocence unhobbled by hard knocks; a fresh, spontaneous mind not fixed in rigid thinking patterns; a time when the border between fantasy and reality was permeable. The fairy tale Dummling is typically open to the unknown, not tied to a rational perspective. In my experience that is an important attitude to adopt in trying to understand dreams and other manifestations of the unconscious. It is also a great help in discovering our own instinct of truth."

"It seems to me," mused Pam, "that the youngest son is closest to the undivided Oneness of the child, so he embodies that child-like spirit of naiveté and adventure that von Franz says is the best way to approach the unconscious."

I cannot tell you how proud I was of her.

"Often in fairy tales the older sons are scornful of the youngest," said Adam, "but here we are told they all love each other. What do you make of that?"

"I suppose brotherly love augers well for a satisfactory resolution in the end," remarked Pam.

"So it does," nodded Adam. "And the Dummling or youngest brother is the hero figure who can put things right."

I had been browsing among the books and now spoke up: "Listen to what von Franz says about this":

> The hero is the restorer of the healthy, conscious situation. He is the one ego that restores to healthy, normal functioning a situation in which all the egos of that tribe or nation are deviating from their instinctive, basic totality pattern. It can therefore he said that *the hero is an archetypal figure which presents a model of an ego functioning in accord with the Self.* . . . It is a *model* to be looked at, and it is demonstrating a rightly functioning ego, an ego that functions in accordance with the requirements of the Self. In a way, therefore, he is also the Self, because he expresses or incarnates its healing tendencies.[82]

Luigi said: "Might the Dummling-hero not also be viewed psychologically as the inferior function?"

---

[82] *The Interpretation of Fairy Tales,* p. 45.

Clever fellow! Maybe in the down-times between cooking my meals and ironing my shirts he'd been reading Jung, or even my book on types, where I say that in a one-sided person the inferior function has the energy required by consciousness for a harmonious, well-balanced perspective.[83] I believe that, though I may have cribbed it from Jung or von Franz.

"From what little I know of it," said Luigi, "one-sidedness is a primary symptom of neurosis, is it not?"

Adam: "Indeed. That's why a thinking type in a psychological crisis has to work on how he feels, and vice versa, the feeling type needs to call on his thinking function."

"And also why intuitives," I added, "have to develop a better relationship to reality, the here and now, while sensation types need to attend to the possibilities."

"Just so," agreed Adam. He scanned down the page. "And what do you think it means," he asked, "this condition that the two older brothers could appear in their human form for two hours a day?"

There was silence.

I finally said: "Perhaps it suggests that the situation is not irredeemable. The number two, although it's a feminine digit—they're in the power of the negative mother, after all—also represents polarity and conflict. My experience, for what it's worth, is that consciousness is not possible without conflict. I've even noticed that people who come into analysis without a conflict soon develop one. So from this point of view, the older brothers are two psychic elements in conflict—let's say they're two complexes at odds with each other, for that's what it comes down to in a real life. The youngest brother is then 'the third'—the transcendent function[84]—which would be the heroic attitude of consciousness required to redeem the situation."

"I like that!" beamed Pam.

---

[83] *Personality Types*, pp. 21ff.

[84] Jung believed that if one consciously holds the tension between opposites in a conflict situation, then the resolution, an irrational "third" (the transcendent function) would be constellated, typically manifesting as a new attitude.

"Makes sense to me," said Luigi.

I expanded: "As some of you know, in alchemical lore there is an intriguing precept known as the Axiom of Maria. It goes likes this: 'One becomes two, two becomes three, and out of the third comes the one as the fourth.'[85] Jung saw this dictum as an apt metaphor for the process of individuation, a progressive advance of consciousness in which conflict plays a profoundly important part."

Pam said: "Would you mind spelling that out?"

I didn't mind at all.

"In brief," I said, "*one* stands for the original, paradisiacal state of unconscious wholeness (for instance, childhood); *two* signifies the conflict between opposites (ego and shadow, say); *three* points to a potential resolution; *the third* is the transcendent function; and *the one as the fourth* is alchemical code for the Philosophers' Stone—psychologically equivalent to a transformed state of consciousness, relatively whole and at peace. Put it this way: you go around the block and come back to square one, knowing rather more about yourself than when you started."

That was a lot to take in. Luigi went off to brew coffee and Adam sorted papers. Pam and I swam in each other's eyes. Sigh. I can tell you, being a romantic in this day and age may buck the trend, but it sure is a lot of fun.

Pumped up with caffeine, we got back to business.

Adam said: "The two brothers and two hours a day point to the doubling motif, which von Franz says refers to something just coming up to the threshold of consciousness. In the unconscious, you see, the opposites are contained as one; only when a particular content crosses the threshold of consciousness does it polarize into two, and therefore engender a conflict.[86] Can you think of an example?"

"Well," I said, "Jung was fond of referring to the Biblical parable of

---

[85] *Psychology and Alchemy,* CW 12, par. 26. My daughter Jessy Kate has this axiom tattooed on her left shoulder, in Greek. For sure it was not my doing.

[86] See *On Divination and Synchronicity: The Psychology of Meaningful Chance,* pp. 105ff.

Buridan's ass, the donkey who starved to death between two piles of hay because he couldn't make a choice. Jung said the important thing was not which bundle was better, or which one he ought to eat first, but what he wanted in the depths of his being—which did he feel pushed toward?"[87]

"How about adultery?" asked Pam. "As long as the right hand isn't aware of what the left hand is doing, there'd be no conflict. But when you become truly conscious of your actions, or maybe even fantasize about, for instance, having an extramarital affair, then a moral conflict—between right and wrong—would be constellated, right?"

It wasn't hard to guess where that came from, but of course I did not let on.

Adam smiled at Pam. "Good for you. I can only point out that what is right for one may be wrong for another."

I plowed ahead.

"The youngest son, then," I said, "fearing that his enchantress mother might change him into a bear or a lion—which is to say bewitch him, like his unfortunate brothers—sets out in search of the princess in the Castle of the Golden Sun. Perhaps the mythological paradigm here is Hercules, who was driven mad by his negative mother Hera—he was in fact overwhelmed by his animal instincts—and in his rage massacred his wife and children. His subsequent deeds in search of redemption marked him as the greatest hero of Greece. That's an example of how the negative feminine can be teleologically positive: the 'bad mother' drives a man out of the nest in search of his soul—the 'princess' who personifies his inner other, a.k.a. the anima, who presumably would depotentiate the power of the witch."

I was on a roll and could hardly stop for breath.

"In the heavenly Jerusalem the castle is a symbol of the transcendent soul. In Kafka's novel *The Castle,* it has been interpreted as a symbol of divine grace . . ."

Pam nodded: "Traditionally the castle is a container, a positive feminine symbol."

---

[87] "The Structure of the Unconscious," *Two Essays,* CW 7, par. 487.

"Yes," I said excitedly, "and here, associated with the Golden Sun, it is connected with masculine symbolism, namely the light of higher consciousness, a potential gift of the anima in her role as Sophia, or Wisdom in the Bible. So the castle in the tale represents a union of opposites. That's what our Dummling-hero is after: the *mysterium coniunctionis!*"

"That's a stretch," said Luigi.

Pam looked at him.

"It's a small world if you don't stretch," she smiled.

Adam asked, "And what about the twenty-three youths who according to the tale have already died a miserable death trying to free the princess?"

"Well," I said, "that could reflect the empirical fact that many attempts to storm the inner citadel are necessary before the anima becomes the helpful mediator between a man's conscious ego and his unconscious—which Jung maintains is her proper function psychologically. It just means that a man has to pay constant attention to his feelings and emotions; that's what brings his anima into the picture. And since she often acts like another person with a will of her own, he can even have a dialogue with her."

Pam said: "There's a parallel with the hundreds of knights who die trying to rescue the princess in the Polish tale 'The Glass Mountain,' and also with the ninety-seven princes who lose their heads trying to win the beautiful princess in another Grimm tale, 'The Sea Hare.' "

Well, I don't know how much of that came from her night course, but you can't say she hadn't done her homework.

Something else occurred to me.

"Hey folks, twenty-three is a prime number; it can only be divided by one and itself. Psychologically that suggests an intransigent complex, one that can't be broken down into smaller parts more easily dealt with."

"But listen," said Luigi, "perhaps it is actually twenty-two plus one—the one who survived to tell the tale . . . ."

"Good thinking!" I cried. "And twenty-two is the circumference of a circle, ubiquitous symbol of wholeness, whose diameter is 'holy

seven'—pi x 7 = 22—again suggesting that the situation is not entirely lost."

"Let's read on," sighed Adam, and he did:

> [The youth] had traveled about for a long time without being able to find
> it [the Castle of the Golden Sun], when he came by chance into a great
> forest, and did not know the way out of it. All at once he saw in the dis-
> tance two giants, who made a sign to him with their hands, and when he
> came to them they said: "We are quarelling about a cap, and which of us it
> is to belong to, and as we are equally strong, neither of us can get the bet-
> ter of the other. The small men are cleverer than we are, so we will leave
> the decision to you."

"Any thoughts?" asked Adam.

"The forest," I said, "as a dark and moist place, shielded by foliage
from the light of the sun, is a frequent symbol of the unconscious in
dreams, legends and fairy tales. Being trapped in the forest is a variant
of the night-sea journey motif, symbolizing a descent into the unconscious. In real life this would likely manifest as depression, a lack of
energy. It is psychologically equivalent to what primitives called loss
of soul, an expression we still use today to describe how a man might
feel when he has no contact with his inner woman."

Adam nodded: "The terrors and monsters in a real forest represent
the perilous aspects of the unconscious—if one goes in and doesn't
come out, it is tantamount to schizophrenia."

I had a lot to say about giants, like how in fairy tales they are generally stupid louts who guard the treasure or princess. Psychologically
they represent complexes associated with strong emotions. The
Dummling-hero's task is often to make friends with them so they become helpers instead of standing in his way. I could also do a number
on the psychological significance of the cap or hat, which with its
round crown has been described at some length by Jung as a symbol of
the Self,[88] and, as a container for thoughts, symbolically analogous to
the alchemical vessel of transformation.

---

[88] *Psychology and Alchemy,* CW 12, pars. 52f.

Alas, I did not get a chance to continue strutting my stuff. It was close to noon so we took a break for lunch: egg rolls, cucumber and avocado sandwiches, iced tea and Luigi's apple strudel with whipped cream—to which I added a liter of an Italian red, Montepulciano d'Abruzzo, 2001. Not the healthiest combination of foods, perhaps— especially not for an O-positive blood type, as I am, or for Adam, who suffered from a chronic condition of atrial fibrillation due to a bout of rheumatic fever as a child—but surely one of the tastiest.

"And how was your time by the sea, my dear?" asked Adam of Pam, referring to her recent holiday.

"So-so," she said with a shrug and a slight wince. "Maybe I was ex- pecting too much."

She did not elaborate and Adam didn't pursue it. Nor would I, at least not in front of the others.

Luigi put his oar between them: "Say, why are Jungians so inter- ested in fairy tales anyway?"

Adam considered.

"Because in fairy tales," he said, "one can best study the compara- tive anatomy of the psyche. It is also useful practice for interpreting dream images and motifs objectively, rather than referring them to some event or situation in the life of the dreamer. The more familiar analysts become with archetypal motifs as they appear in myths, fairy tales, legends and dreams, the better equipped they are to under- stand what is going on psychologically in those they work with."

"And for those who aren't analysts," I added, "they can just better understand themselves—if they have a mind to."

Okay, so that was a stretch too, but I believed it to be so.

There was more small talk and we got set to continue with the tale, when suddenly Adam sighed as if he were about to give up the ghost.

"Don't know about you," he said, "but I've had the biscuit. Let's call it a day."

We readily agreed to continue another time.

Well, as it happens we didn't, for my life took an unexpected turn.

11
Momma Mia

About a week after that fairy tale workshop I fell into one of those potholes I mentioned way back when—a deep, deep depression. It came out of the blue and laid me low. It just happened; from one day to the next I found myself in a funk. Oh, on the outside I was cheery as ever and I took care of business well enough, but inside I was curled up like a fetus. I hurt; it was worse than a tooth-ache.

"Momma mia!" I cried silently, "Where are you?"

Understand now, I didn't wail for my personal mother. She was long gone. The mum I called for was the mother of invention, of creativity, the mother of the not-yet-known, mother of what was yet to be: my inner, archetypal mother. In short, the Great Mother.

I was at the end of my tether. I didn't know what to do next, what to write, how to be. I took to roaming the streets again, looking for action, popping in and out of pubs. I kept an eye out for someone to sparkle with and came upon more than a few who were willing, but then I wasn't. Pam was in my head all the time. I was the life of any party, but I drank too much and didn't sleep well.

Talk about regression, I was in it up to my ears. The feeling that I was a turd came back, together with a touch of paranoia—I imagined someone was out to get me. I had dreams where I was at pains to stop young hooligans and homeless people from breaking into my house. I took that to mean I was trying to avoid dealing with something, but what? I didn't have a clue.

An analysand of mine once gave me an image of how he felt when he was out of touch with who he was. He said he saw himself as a walking deck of cards, continually being shuffled, and he never knew which card was going to be up front from one minute to the next. I felt I was going through something similar; I was a feckless chameleon, endlessly shuffling fifty-two personas.

When I realized what was happening, namely that I had lost contact with my center (call it the Self, okay), I resolved to do just as in my practice I often counsel others.

Instead of trying to escape the depression, I sank into it. I stopped my party-going and went into seclusion. I introspected. I even stayed away from Adam and Pam, missing them like crazy, but what can you do. I depended on Luigi; he did the shopping and made the meals. I holed up and focused on what ailed me. I did not leave my house for two weeks other than to pick up the mail each day at eight a.m., a routine so ingrained in me over the past twenty-five years that if I stopped doing that I might as well call it quits.

I turned a searchlight on my innards by writing, painting and playing with clay. I took up knitting. I made mittens for my wee grandson Devon, whose month-old fist was hardly bigger than my thumb. I knit a toque for my gargoyle Arnold; it was full of holes, which I called *yonis,* just for the fun of it.[89]

I made copious notes on how I felt. I personified my complexes and talked to them. That was, after all, how I got out of the hole I was in so many years ago when I first ran afoul of myself and realized the urgent need to change.[90]

The object of this kind of activity, which Jung called active imagination, is to give a voice to sides of the personality that one is ordinarily not in touch with; in other words, the aim is to establish a line of communication between consciousness and the unconscious. This is a delicate, ongoing process. It is not necessary to interpret the drawings or paintings, etc., no need to figure out what they mean. You do them and you live with them. Something goes on between you and what you create. And it doesn't need to be put into words to be effective. In fact, sometimes articulating what you think they mean even interferes with the process.

I browsed in many books looking for answers, advice, all that. I found a passage in Storr's *Solitude* that gave me pause for thought:

---

[89] In Hindu religious art and worship, the *lingam-yoni* dyad symbolizes the male and female sex organs, respectively.

[90] See *The Survival Papers: Anatomy of a Midlife Crisis,* pp. 131ff.

It seems probable that there is always an element of play in creative living. When this playful element disappears, joy goes with it, and so does any sense of being able to innovate. Creative people not infrequently experience periods of despair in which their ability to create anything new seems to have deserted them. This is often because a particular piece of work has become invested with such overwhelming importance that it is no longer possible to play with it.[91]

Good grief! Had I not been playing enough with my "particular piece of work"? Or perhaps too much? Judge for yourself; if you've read this far you have a right to say. As for me, I was baffled.

In Warren Steinberg's *Circle of Care* I came upon comments that served to remind me of Jung's views:

Jung saw a relationship between depression and transformation, and was primarily interested in applying his ideas about depression to the study of this relationship. For him the unconscious is creative; that is, it produces contents whose purpose is the development of the personality. The need to become aware of these issues may deprive the ego of energy and result in depression. In this case the depression is not a pathological reaction but a natural consequence of the inner need for transformation. . . .

In transformative depressions, libido is attracted by some psychic content that needs to become conscious in order to further the individuation process. This form of depression is purposive. . . . In order to recover the lost energy one must look into the unconscious and find what has attracted the energy. This attracting force will appear in the form of a fantasy or image. If the individual can bring up and integrate the images that attract and hold the libido, energy will again become available to ego-consciousness.[92]

Well said! In other words, being depressed is not necessarily a sign of neurosis. Steinberg also points out that according to M. Esther Harding, what I was going through might even be called a "creative depression."[93] Thanks for that, it gave me heart. It's not that I

---

[91] *Solitude,* pp. 71f.

[92] *Circle of Care: Clinical Issues in Jungian Therapy,* pp. 120f.

[93] See Harding, "The Meaning and Value of Depression."

wasn't aware of the possibility, but being of an age when the synapses aren't synapsing as they used to, I am always grateful to be reminded of what I once knew, which by a fluke of nature I have forgotten.

I went to Jung's Collected Works, where I found more reminders, especially of the need to become aware of where my energy naturally wanted to go:

> What is it, at this moment and in this individual, that represents the natural urge of life? That is the question.
>
> That question neither science, nor worldly wisdom, nor religion, nor the best of advice can resolve for him. The resolution can come solely from absolutely impartial observation of those psychological germs of life which are born of the natural collaboration of the conscious and the unconscious on the one hand and of the individual and the collective on the other. Where do we find these germs of life? One man seeks them in the conscious, another in the unconscious. But the conscious is only one side, and the unconscious is only its reverse.[94]

> Psychic energy is a very fastidious thing which insists on fulfilment of its own conditions. However much energy may be present, we cannot make it serviceable until we have succeeded in finding the right gradient.[95]

> There is no energy unless there is a tension of opposites; hence it is necessary to discover the opposite to the attitude of the conscious mind. . . . The repressed content must be made conscious so as to produce a tension of opposites, without which no forward movement is possible. The conscious mind is on top, the shadow underneath, and just as high always longs for low and hot for cold, so all consciousness, perhaps without being aware of it, seeks its unconscious opposite . . . . Life is born only of the spark of opposites.[96]

Well, that reference to sparks really hit me because, frankly, it brought to mind the ongoing attraction between Pam and me. I already knew we were typological opposites. So, where there are sparks, is there fire?

---

[94] *Two Essays,* CW 7, pars. 488f.

[95] Ibid., par. 76.

[96] Ibid., par. 78.

Elsewhere Jung compares the flow of energy to a river:

The libido has, as it were, a natural penchant: it is like water, which must have a gradient if it is to flow.[97]

Hmmm. Double hmmm. Okay, so where did my energy want to go—its natural gradient—and what was the opposite of my conscious attitude? I choked a glass with ice, filled it with single malt and settled in to ruminate. I thought of Bogey's famous remark: "The world is always three drinks behind." Well, I wasn't about to let it catch up.

And then Rachel was there, up front and center.

"Oh, so glad to see you!" I said.

What an understatement. I am embarrassed to say that when I'm depressed I tend to forget about Rachel. Luckily she isn't so fickle. This was not the first time she had appeared without being conjured up by me. I don't mind, I'd just like to know how she does it.

She was in her classically demure outfit: long black skirt and white blouse with cuff ruffles and high collar, black lace-up boots. Her hair flowed auburn and there was a red rose tucked over her left ear. She looked adorably Renaissance. Botticelli's "Primavera" came to mind. I felt I was in the presence of a goddess.

I fell to my knees and sobbed.

Rachel stamped her foot and clapped her hands. "Stop it!" she said.

I peered up at her. "Pardon me?"

"I am not your Holy Mother Mary Immaculate, free of body and sinless. I am Mary Magdalene, if anyone, and my past is not your business."

This was new. Mary Magdalene?! Give me a break. I sat up and pulled myself together, again. The trick in dealing with Rachel, or better said, the way to get the most from an encounter with her, is not to question what she says and not to accuse her of being inflated, but simply to accept with good grace her presumption of authority.

"For weeks now you have been moaning and groaning," she said. "What's up?"

---

[97] *Symbols of Transformation,* CW 5, par. 337.

Well, I could tell her what wasn't, but even with Rachel I don't get that intimate. Full disclosure has a limit.

"I need help," I confessed.

"State your case."

Holy Toledo, now she was in her judge's robes, snow-white blouse under black crepe down to the floor. "She who must be obeyed!"[98] My heart fell. We had been here before and she had ruled against me, implicitly suggesting that one day, if I diligently worked on myself and religiously kept track of my dreams, I would become whole again, as when I was an innocent five year old who believed in Santa Claus and the Easter Bunny and thought God made all the houses and the trees, and had no idea where babies came from. This is a recurring fantasy of mine, which I can't seem to shake. At the same time, I don't have to believe it.

So, telling myself that I was now a grown-up, I resolved to defend myself without being defensive.

"Rachel," I said, feeling that it was time to let it out, "Do you recall the ball dream that took me into analysis?"

"My memory," she sniffed, "is probably better than that of any of the hundred or so elephants on your mantelpiece."

Okay, so she was having her fun with me. I played along.

"Well, just to remind myself, then, It went like this":

I am on a street in the center of a deserted city, surrounded by cavernous buildings. I am bouncing a ball between the buildings, from one side to another. It kept getting away from me, I could not pin it down. I woke up in a cold sweat, terrified, sobbing uncontrollably.

That was my initial dream, as we say—the first one I took to an analyst. From this distance it seems quite innocuous, but at the time it

---

[98] Jung often used this moniker to characterize the inner authority of the anima. He picked it up from H. Rider Haggard's 1887 novel, *She*. (See, for instance, *Two Essays*, CW 7, pars. 298f.) The expression, "She who must be obeyed," was popularized in the 1980s by the British television series, *Rumpole of Walpole Street*, in which the attorney Horace Rumpole was pictured as forever under the thumb of his wife. My own experience is that the anima has the upper hand only when her views are not attended to. After that you can have a dialogue without being concerned about who's winning.

had such a powerful effect on me that it utterly changed my life. It was my introduction to the reality of the psyche, a kind of initiation, a baptism by fire.

Before that ball dream, I did not know that something could be going on in me without my being aware of it. I was a child of the Enlightenment, after all. My primary education was in maths and physics. I prided myself on being rational and I had barely heard of the unconscious, let alone believed in it. I was certain that will power could accomplish anything. At the time of that dream I was a privileged employee in a major corporation. I had a key to the executive washroom and stock options. I loved what I was doing and on my desk was a sign stating my credo: "Where there's a will there's a way."

My dream of the bouncing ball came in the midst of a personal conflict which I had a will to solve, but no way. I kept thinking that I could deal with it by myself. My reaction to the dream—the tears that wouldn't stop, the sleepless nights that followed—destroyed that illusion. I realized that I really had only two options: to blow my brains out or go into analysis. I chose the latter; lucky me, still alive after all these years.

Rachel was forgiving, as usual. I mean she did not give me a hard time for imagining she might forget such a landmark dream. And she didn't judge me at all. I don't know for sure, but it is quite possible that I project onto her—my own anima!—a critical attitude in order to compensate for my positive mother complex. Hmmm. I will look into that when I have some time off from so much else to do.

"As I recall," said Rachel. "we came to see that dream in terms of the difficulty you were then having in keeping the opposites in balance. We saw the ball as a symbol for self-containment, and the intent of the dream as evidence for the ongoing, self-regulating process in the psyche. The fact that the ball kept getting away from you underlined the fact that you were not in control. Right?"

I nodded. It was all coming back to me.

"Yes, oh yeah," I said. "I was bursting out in all directions, not at all contained. I was the epitome of collective man. My bible was Dale Carnegie's *How to Win Friends and Influence People*. I was extremely extraverted, hail fellow well met. I did not have a thought I could call my own and no personal center. I had a wife and three children and more girl-friends than Hugh Hefner. I grew my own Fineglow in our suburban vegetable patch, right behind the corn. I got high at a Rolling Stones concert and fell into bed with my secretary. My life was so compartmentalized that I didn't have a clue who was me."

I put my head down and wept.

Rachel said: "Okay, okay, now listen up. Stop beating yourself to pieces for who you once were. That was then and today is now. We have work to do. What is currently going on in your life that is in some way similar to what you went through thirty years ago? What change are you resisting?"

Well, that was a toughy, no kidding.

I mopped up my tears and wracked my brain. Nothing came to mind. I mean, thirty years ago I was on my knees. Now I wasn't, and hadn't been for as long as I could remember. Sure, from time to time I hobble along with sore legs, a back-ache or stiff neck, but who doesn't; stress is the price we pay for being civilized. There are so many palliatives for our physical ailments—and so many views on what causes or cures—that if we took such things to heart we would be walking pharmaceuticals. And diets? Don't get me started. I trust my body and that's my bottom line.

"I leave you to it," said Rachel, and disappeared.

Sometimes she does that. Just when you think she's about to solve all your problems, she goes into hiding. It's really annoying, but she's her own person; that's just the way it is.

Okay, I got down to brass tacks. In order to put into perspective my current situation, I did an inventory of my progression through life, dividing the various stages acronymically as follows:

—PP (prepuberty, about which I remember very little);

—AD (adolescence, when my hormones were so active I could hardly eat);

—YA (young adult, when my hormones were so active I would have a go at a chicken);

—PR (parental responsibilities, which I thoroughly enjoyed);
—PM (post-marriage, which I enjoyed even more);
—FMV (finding my vocation, which has since sustained me).

Overall, the major divisions in my life have been BA (Before Analysis) and AA (After Analysis). Of what went on in the BA period, I often need to be reminded, which my now grown-up children are not loath to do—though kindly, I should say, without acrimony. The AA period usually takes care of itself, being well represented in terms of my current activities—writing and publishing books and practicing as an analyst.

Anyway, the point I meant to make before I got sidetracked is that life is now so complicated and we're bombarded with so much pain and sorrow in the world that we can't do a single thing about—well, without donating our whole net worth to some relief agency, still a drop in the bucket even if our $$$ get by corrupt officials and reach their destination, meanwhile reducing our own life to zero—that it's a wonder we can function at all. Just to read the daily newspaper would reduce a statue to tears. Life didn't used to be so difficult. Now there is so much incoming information that it is crazy making. I hope my kids can keep up with it, because I can't.

There, I was off track again. Where was I, oh yes, Rachel's query: What is going on now that is similar to what brought me to my knees so many years ago? What change might I be resisting? They were questions that I took to heart.

There was so much going on in my head and my house that I had to get away to come to grips with an answer. I booked a room in a posh lodge on Georgian Bay in northern Ontario and settled in. I took my dog-eared traveling set of Jung's Collected Works, which I never go anywhere without, and a few pot-boilers just in case. I took my Walkman and a bunch of CD's. I did not take my lap-top Mac and I didn't call in for messages. Every morning I did lengths in the pool and then lay back in the hot tub. I had a daily massage and Alicia gave me my first-ever pedicure. I wallowed in good mother.

I stayed there for seven days and seven nights. I went for walks and stared at the wall. I had several conversations with Rachel, who was more than helpful. It was off-season, so there weren't many other guests. I dined and chatted with a Japanese couple and an old gent who lost a leg in the Second World War. I did not come across any lovelies (well, other than the fair Alicia, honor bound not to frolic with her clients); lucky me again, because for sure that would have distracted me from what I was there for.

Over and over I listened to Frank Sinatra belting out love songs.

> *Never thought I'd fall,*
> *But now I hear love's call.*
> *I'm getting sentimental over you.*
> *Things you say and do,*
> *Just thrill me through and through,*
> *I'm getting sentimental over you.*[99]

And this:

> *Do you love me, as I love you,*
> *Are you my life to be, my dream come true,*
> *Or will this dream of mine*
> *Fade out of sight*
> *Like the moon growing dim,*
> *On the rim of the hill*
> *In the chill, chill, chill, still of the night.*[100]

By the end of the week I knew what I had to do. Like a general marshaling his forces, I laid out a plan of action. I felt good. I slept easy. I could smile again.

Back in the city, I took steps to make actual what for me was truly an unexpected enantiodromia—the emergence of the unconscious opposite in the course of time. Or you can call it the transcendent function, that's true too.

Timing is everything. *Kairos.*

---

[99] Lyrics by George Bassman and Ned Washington.
[100] Lyrics by Arthur Schwartz and Howard Dietz.

12
Ballin' the Jack

"Marriage is rather more than dinner and a movie," remarked Pam, picking at her organic baby spinach leaves, generously dressed with triple virgin olive oil and balsamic vinegar.

We were having lunch at Fleshless, an aptly named vegetarian restaurant that served nothing to my liking. I ate the several soy-based dishes anyway because I had been told by someone, or maybe I read somewhere, that they were good for me.[101]

"Yes," I smiled, "I've been there." As if she didn't know.

"You're sure about this?"

"I am."

Pam shook her head. "But I'm already married!"

"That can be undone," I said.

"You're asking me to leave my husband of twenty-two years and be with you?"

"That is so," I said.

Her voice rose. "And we haven't even slept together?! Are you out of your friggin' mind?!"

Heads turned in our direction. I waved a smile to them. I turned to Pam and pulled out my three jacks and the two and the five. I fanned them on the table. I lifted Pam's right hand to my lips.

"Can you beat that? I love you, for what it's worth."

Yeah, so it was corny, but it felt good to say it.

Pam flicked her wrist and eyed me. She didn't say No.

"So how come this change of heart? You've told me that you like being single and living alone, and you've said as much in some of your books too. So what's happened?"

"*You* happened," I said. "It's true that I like having my own space.

---

[101] That's the power of a mother complex big as a house, in tandem with a three-bedroom condo of a father complex. They get you coming and going.

But my proposal doesn't necessarily involve living together. I am a great fan of intimacy with distance, which refers not to geographic but psychological separation—knowing where you end and the other begins.[102] If we can manage that, it doesn't matter whether we live together or not. And of course we could be with each other whenever we felt like it anyway, that goes without saying."

I choked down another kamut noodle.

"Actually, the real change in me—call it an epiphany if you want, for that is how it feels—is realizing that you are my true bride."[103]

Pam wrung her hands and trembled. Her eyes leaked. She put her fork down.

"Slow down, okay? This is very sudden. I need time to get my head around it. What you and I have together is very precious to me. It's true that I'm not completely satisfied with the life I have, but on the whole it's workable. My kids would go bananas if they knew I wasn't who they think I am. My husband? Well, he depends on me to be there for him, and if I wasn't I'm afraid he'd fall apart."

Pam cupped my head in her hands. "Why can't we just continue to have fun being loverNots?"

It was a fair question. Her fears—how others would react if she followed her heart—were not groundless. On the other hand, as I saw it, the bigger question was one of personal authenticity and how far one should go in assuming responsibility for the lives of others, when our concern for their welfare might abort or interfere with our own process of individuation, and, as a matter of fact, might hinder theirs as well. In my own experience, falling apart was the best thing that ever happened to me.

I also wondered: to what or to whom is our primary responsibility owed? Is focusing on our own wants and needs selfish or simply good

---

[102] See, for instance, "Togetherness vs. Intimacy with Distance," in my *Digesting Jung: Food for the Journey,* pp. 67ff.

[103] The psychological significance of the true bride vs. the false bride—a prominent motif in many fairy tales—is explored in my *Dear Gladys: The Survival Papers, Book 2,* pp. 124ff.

mental hygiene? When, if ever, should we accept that we are captains
of only our own journey, and that others are captains of theirs?[104] I
don't mind crewing for others—that's part and parcel of my vocation, after all—but their captain? No, not my job.

Such sticky issues.

Pam and I had been seeing each other regularly for more than a
year, and we had exchanged many a *billet doux*. From the very first
there were fireworks between us, but we had contained them. We had
held the tension. I couldn't speak for her, but from my side there were
now fewer projections. I had a much better idea of who she was, as
opposed to who I thought she was when we first met. In other words, I
had a good handle on the difference between her and Pam2. I could
appreciate her as someone wonderfully other, and I could imagine being with her forever, for better or worse, come rain or come shine.

A romantic idea, for sure, but listen, it's better than the big sleep.

As far as I knew, Pam's husband was completely in the dark about
the relationship that had developed between Pam and I. As a matter
of fact, I sympathized with him because I too had been blind-sided
when my partner of more than twenty years left me for someone
else. In time I got over my hurt, as I imagined Pam's husband would;
well, if she decided to leave him—for me or for herself, same difference—which at this point was only a possibility. But if she did, maybe
he would start wondering who he was, really. Like I said, falling apart
was the best thing that ever happened to me. Maybe it would change
his life too.

Anyway, that wasn't my business. I had declared myself to Pam,
that's where we were at. And she still hadn't said No.

Betrayal! That motif came to mind. How we betray our loved ones
in spite of loving them, or maybe even because of. Betrayal is the opposite of trust. I remembered an interesting essay on the subject by
James Hillman, and right there, in this meatless restaurant, a passage
from it popped into my head:

---

[104] I was thinking here of James Hollis's recent book, *On This Journey We Call Our
Life: Living the Questions.*

We can be truly betrayed only where we truly trust—by brothers, lovers, wives, husbands, not by enemies, not by strangers. The greater the love and loyalty, the involvement and commitment, the greater the betrayal. Trust has in it the seed of betrayal; the serpent was in the garden from the beginning, just as Eve was pre-formed in the structure around Adam's heart. Trust and the possibility of betrayal come into the world at the same moment. Wherever there is trust in a union, the risk of betrayal becomes a real possibility. And betrayal, as a continual possibility to be lived with, belongs to trust just as doubt belongs to a living faith.[105]

I was almost crying, not sure why.

I'd been quiet for so long that Pam poked me. "Dear one, are those tears? What's that about?"

I took out a handkerchief and dabbed at my eyes. "Sorry, I went into never-never land. You were saying?"

And she asked again: "Why don't we just go on being loverNots? We have wonderful fun when we're together, right? We always find something to sing about. Our hearts seem to open and overlap in special places when we play. What we have is really good. Could it be even better? I don't know! It might be worse! I am really scared of what might happen."

Hey, that was usually my line. So, it seemed that as I was becoming more comfortable with the unknown and possibilities, Pam the intuitive was moving away from them. I saw that as another example of enantiodromia.

I pulled myself together, which—it suddenly struck me—I had been doing rather a lot lately. Hmmm, perhaps in a compensatory effort not to fall apart? But I just said that falling apart had been good for me, so why would I resist it now?! Why not let go and see how far down was bottom?

. . . "Do I dare?" and, "Do I dare?"
Time to turn back and descend the stair,
With a bald spot in the middle of my hair— . . .
I grow old . . . I grow old . . .

---

[105] "Betrayal," in *Loose Ends,* p. 66.

I shall wear the bottoms of my trousers rolled.
Shall I part my hair behind? Do I dare to eat a peach?[106]

So many questions, so few answers.

Okay, all I knew for sure was that I had been under a cloud for so long that the sun was just a rumor. But today the skies had cleared and I was more or less myself. At least I knew what I wanted. I hoped that gave me an advantage in courting fair lady.

I once read somewhere—or it could be I even wrote it myself—that the quintessential mark of masculinity is knowing what you want and doing what is necessary in order to get it. If that is true, which granted it might not be, that's where I was, willy-nilly.

"Well," I said to Pam, "what we now have is fun, that's for sure, but I'm feeling it's no longer enough for me. Think of it. We are a community of two. We have to hide our affection from those who know us, and we're always having to think of who we might run into when we venture out. We have a peek-a-boo relationship. We are loverNots, which is great as far as it goes, but for all the secrecy we might as well be lovers."

She bit her lip, listening.

"Pam, dear heart, *anam cara*, I want us to be together in the eyes of others. I want us to be seen. Also, I have to say," and here I wriggled a bit, "being celibate is getting me down. It's just not me. I long to tryst and shout."

She leaned over and whispered: "You could bonk someone else, I'd be okay with that."

Yeah, I bet.

Was it not ever thus? I did not fool myself that what was going on between Pam and me was in any way unique. Nowadays it's the norm at midlife to fancy someone new. If you can stay with your original partner for ten years, say, count yourself a champ. After twenty years, you deserve a medal. At thirty, you get your picture taken with

---

[106] T.S. Eliot, "The Love Song of J. Alfred Prufrock," in *The Complete Poems and Plays of T. S. Eliot,* lines 38-40, 120-122.

the mayor. At forty the governor checks in. At fifty . . . well, long before that, like as not you've been tearing your hair, so bored with your mate that you long for separate holidays.

Okay, everyone over the age of puberty knows that being crazy in love doesn't last forever. But you know what? That's no reason not to respond to sparks, Cupid's arrow, the tug of Eros, at any age. Being in love might in time become loving, a relationship beyond projection, where the other is accepted as he or she really is. And if it doesn't, *c'est la vie,* try another experiment in living your life, which at my age you know is going to end sooner rather than later.

Jeez, I was beginning to sound like Adam.

Pam and I gazed at each other for a long while. We moved into a liminal space where only the two of us existed. It was quite an extraordinary feeling. The ambient music was Rod Stewart singing his heart out, synchronistically echoing what was going on in me:

> *You go to my head, and you linger like a haunting refrain*
> *And I find you spinning 'round in my brain*
> *Like the bubbles in a glass of champagne . . .*
>
> *The thrilll of the thought that you might give a thought to my plea*
> *Cast a spell over me.*
> *Like a summer with a thousand Julys*
> *You intoxicate my soul with your eyes.*[107]

Pam blinked first.

"Okay, okay!" she said, tossing her napkin on the table, like a gauntlet. "Supposing I were to leave my husband and my life as I know it, which I'm nowhere near doing, understand, but just supposing, right, just supposing?"

I took her hands in mine. "Yes, go on."

Pam laughed her signature tinkle. "What's this marriage business anyway? Why couldn't we just be common-law partners?"

"It is a possibility," I said. "I've been there too, and it was pretty good. But maybe going the whole hog would be better."

---

[107] "You Go to My Head," lyrics by Haven Gillespie and J. Fred Coots.

Pam was quiet as our waitress came and cleared the table.

"You guys finished?" she asked.

"Just starting," I smiled. "But bring the bill-ball, thanks."

Pam leaned forward: "Do you have in mind some grand ceremony? Like tying the knot at the top of the CN Tower? So we could call ourselves loverKnots . . . ?"

LoverKnots! See what I mean?

We both laughed.

"No, just my kids and yours, a few close friends. An intimate non-event with no reporters. Promise."

Pam shook her curls and caressed the dung-beetle brooch I had given her for her birthday. So sweet of her to wear it when we were together. I saw it as an apotropaic amulet to chase away evil spirits that might get in the way of our feelings for each other.

"And what else," she smiled.

"Okay, think about this," I said, winging it. "I could abduct you, take you to my underworld den in the bowels of the Hummingbird Center, like the phantom of that opera. There I would ravish you to pieces with no one the wiser. There is no telephone or e-mail in my underworld den, no fax, no cell-phone, not even a computer. On top of that there are no windows and hardly any light at all, only a few candles. It is a shadowy realm for sure, where anything can happen. All told, it's a pretty creepy place."

Pam clapped her hands. "Sounds like fun! I could go for that. It would sure be a lot less disruptive!"

We hugged and kissed, leaving our balls in the air.

That was okay with me. My proposal was unexpected, after all. From Pam's point of view, my professed change of attitude might be just so much doo-doo. If I were her, I would be pretty suspicious.

I dropped Pam off to take her shift at the nursing home. At my place I rang for Luigi.

"You called, sir?"

He was ram-rod perfect, never one to take advantage of our social times together, as when we worked on that fairy tale.

"A six-ounce rib-eye, if you please, plus a lite Caesar salad and rye bread, lightly toasted, unsalted butter. Around six?"

"It shall be done."

"Oh, and Luigi, I'd like you to join me, okay? And open a couple of bottles of Dingbat. I have something to tell you."

"Very good, sir, very very good."

It wasn't yet three p.m. I undressed and lay down for a bit of shut-eye, as I usually do around that time of day. I slept and had a dream. It went something like this:

Balls! Row upon row of balls. Baseballs, basketballs, golf balls, soccer balls, tennis balls, volley balls, snooker balls and more—they stretched out to the horizon as far as I could see. They were lined up in orderly ranks, as on a parade ground. They did not bounce and they did not roll. They *quivered.* There was a magnificent, low-pitched *thrum, thrum,* in the air, which I could not but relate to the music of the spheres.

I appeared on a podium in an officer's uniform and spoke to them through some kind of bull-horn.

"Balls, hear this! I am very proud of you. You did your duty as you saw it. You did not play favorites and you did not stint. You were not major players, but as supporting actors you deserve an Academy Award."

I saluted and turned on my heel. *Thrum, thrum.*

I woke up smiling. So did Rachel.

There remained only to put Adam in the picture, or so I thought. A few days later I took him a flagon of single malt Lagavulin for his gullet and a plant of black-eyed Gerber daisies for his bookshelf.

Adam was wonderfully himself, nattily attired as usual, sitting up in bed doing a crossword puzzle.

"Hi there," he said. "What has four letters, starts with t and rhymes with curd?"

"You rascal," I laughed.

We embraced.

"Pam just left," said Adam. "We had an interesting chat. She's in a bit of a turmoil. Your proposal has constellated a serious conflict, where your Don Juan charm didn't."

"Good!" I said. "You know what I think: conflict is a prerequisite for consciousness."

"True enough, and she is working on it. Meanwhile, you would be wise to give her space, not press her."

"Of course," I said, wanting desperately to do the opposite.

"You should also be prepared," said Adam, "for the possibility that she won't jump ship. And so, meanwhile, you might think of your journey over the past year or so as metaphorically analogous to the alchemical Axiom of Maria."[108]

"Oh? How's that?"

Adam ticked it off on his fingers.

"It's simple. You began as *one;* you came to me and we were *two;* then there was Pam, the *third;* and your change of attitude is *the one as the fourth.*"

"And so?" I really felt like a Dummling, no fooling.

Adam sighed. "Put it this way: you've been around the block and you're back to square one, knowing a little more about yourself than when you started."

Whatta guy. He was quoting me almost word for word. That's what you call intrapsychic plagiarism.

Still, I felt a little let down.

"Is that all there is?" I asked plaintively, as if I were Peggy Lee or still looking for that *Big Book* with all the answers.

"Oh laddie," said Adam. "Unhook me, take me out on the patio and we'll talk under the dapples."

*

"Well done," said Rachel. "You finished the book, but not the story. That's a pretty neat trick."

We hugged.

---

[108] See above, p. 97.

Bibliography

Bauer, Jan. *Alcoholism and Women: The Background and the Psychology.* Toronto: Inner City Books, 1982.

Complete Grimm's Fairy Tales. New York: Pantheon Books, 1944.

de Vries, Ad. *Dictionary of Imagery and Symbolism.* Amsterdam: North-Holland Publishing Co., 1974.

Edinger, Edward F. *Melville's Moby-Dick: An American Nekyia.* Toronto: Inner City Books, 1995.

_____. *The Sacred Psyche: A Psychological Approach to the Psalms.* Toronto: Inner City Books, 2004.

Eliot, T.S. *The Complete Poems and Plays of T. S. Eliot.* Boston: Faber, 1969.

Hannah, Barbara. *Jung: His Life and Work (A Biographical Memoir).* New York: Capricorn Books, G.P. Putnam's Sons, 1976.

Harding, M. Esther. "The Meaning and Valaue of Depression." New York: The Analytical Psychology Club, 1970.

_____. *The Parental Image: Its Injury and Reconstruction.* Toronto: Inner City Books, 2003.

Hillman, James. *Loose Ends.* Zurich: Spring Publications, 1975.

Hollis, James. *On This Journey We Call Our Life: Living the Questions.* Toronto: Inner City Books, 2003.

_____. *Swamplands of the Soul: New Life in Dismal Places.* Toronto: Inner City Books, 1996.

Jung, C.G. *The Collected Works* (Bollingen Series XX). 20 vols. Trans. R.F.C. Hull. Ed. H. Read, M. Fordham, G. Adler, Wm. McGuire. Princeton: Princeton University Press, 1953-1979.

_____. *Memories, Dreams, Reflections.* Ed. Aniela Jaffé. New York: Pantheon Books, 1961.

Jackson, Eve. *Food and Tansformation: Imagery and Symbolism of Eating.* Toronto: Inner City Books, 1996.

Kafka, Franz. *The Diaries of Franz Kafka, 1910-1913.* Trans. Joseph Kresh. Ed. Max Brod. London: Martin Secker and Warburg, 1948.

McGuire, William, ed. *The Freud/Jung Letters* (Bollingen Series XCIV). Trans. Ralph Manheim and R.F.C. Hull. Princeton: Princeton University Press, 1974.

O'Donohue, J. *Anam Cara: A Book of Celtic Wisdom.* New York: HarperCollins, 1998.

Onians, R.B. *The Origins of European Thought.* Cambridge, MA: Cambridge University Press, 1951.

Perera, Sylvia Brinton. *The Scapegoat Complex: Toward a Mythology of Shadow and Guilt.* Toronto: Inner City Books, 1986.

Plato. *The Symposium.* Trans. W.R.M. Lamb. Loeb Classical Library. Cambridge, MA: Harvard University Press, 1961.

Sharp, Daryl. *Chicken Little: The Inside Story.* Toronto: Inner City Books, 1993.

_____. *Dear Gladys: The Survival Papers, Bk. 2.* Toronto: Inner City Books, 1989.

_____. *Jung Lexicon: A Primer of Terms and Concepts.* Toronto: Inner City Books, 1991.

_____. *Living Jung: The Good and the Better.* Toronto: Inner City Books, 1996.

_____. *Personality Types: Jung's Model.* Toronto: Inner City Books, 1987.

_____. *The Secret Raven: Conflict and Transformation in the Life of Franz Kafka.* Toronto: Inner City Books, 1980.

_____. *The Survival Papers: Anatomy of a Midlife Crisis.* Toronto: Inner City Books, 1988.

_____. *Who Am I, Really? Personality, Soul and Individuation.* Toronto: Inner City Books, 1995.

Steinberg, Warren. *Circle of Care: Clinical Issues in Jungian Therapy.* Toronto: Inner City Books, 1990.

Storr, Anthony. *Solitude.* London, UK: HarperCollins, 1997.

von Franz, Marie-Louise. *Alchemy: An Introduction to the Symbolism and the Psychology.* Toronto: Inner City Books, 1980.

_____. *Animus and Anima in Fairy Tales.* Toronto: Inner City Books, 2002.

_____. *C.G. Jung: His Myth in Our Time.* Toronto: Inner City Books, 1998.

_____. *The Interpretation of Fairy Tales.* Zurich: Spring Publications, 1973.

_____. *On Divination and Synchronicity.* Toronto: Inner City Books, 1980.

_____. *The Problem of the Puer Aeternus.* Toronto: Inner City Books, 2000.

Wilhelm, Richard, trans. *The I Ching or Book of Changes.* London: Routledge and Kegan Paul, 1968.

Winnicott, D.W. "Transitional Objects and Transitional Phenomena." In *Through Paediatrics to Psycho-Analysis.* London, 1975.

Woodman, Marion. *The Pregnant Virgin: A Process of Psychological Transformation.* Toronto: Inner City Books, 1985.

Yeoman, Ann. *Now or Neverland: Peter Pan and the Myth of Eternal Youth.* Toronto: Inner City Books, 1999.

Index

Entries in *italics* refer to illustrations

abandonment, 10, 67-68, 73-74, 82
active imagination, 30-33, 68, 103
Adam Brillig. *See* Brillig, Adam
adultery, 29, 98
alchemical/alchemy, 70, 75, 92, 97, 100
Alcoholics Anonymous, 63n
alone, being, 31, 68, 70-72, 76
analysis/analyst, 8, 34, 36, 51, 86, 88, 96, 101-102, 110
anam cara, 51-52, 69, 80
anima, 18, 38, 40, 52, 65, 80-81, 92, 98-99, 107n, 108
animus, 38-40, 45, 52, 65, 80, 92
apotropaic, 77, 118
archetypal/archetype(s), 21-23, 38, 40, 101-102
    and instincts, 22, *23*
art, 42- 43
Aussie guru, 27
authenticity, 113
Axiom of Maria, 97, 120

bad and worse, good and better, 31-32
ball(s), 7, 37
    book outline, 11-14
    dream(s) of, 7, 107-108, 119
    as exploded mandalas, 22
    golden, 26
    rolling, 28
    surface area vs. volume, 7, 57-58
    as symbols of wholeness, 21
    as transitional objects, 25
ball game(s), 7, 11-12, 19, *20,* 21, 24-27, 37
    life like a, 19, 51
Bauer, Jan: *Alcoholism and Women,* 63n
beetle, 32, 118
being alone, 70-72
being vs. doing, 32, 35, 40
betrayal, 114-115
Big Book, The, 50, 120
big sleep, 28, 37, 49, 51, 60, 114

Big Sleep, The (film), 15, 54n
biographies of Jung, 29n
Bogart, Humphrey, 15, 54n, 106
book of wisdom, 50, 120
breaking into house, dream of, 102
Brillig, Adam, 9-11, 14-16, 21-29, 60-67, 91-101, 119-120
    Trilogy, 9n, 56
Buffalo Springfield, 81
Buridan's ass, 98

Camilla, 9n
cap, 100
Carnegie, Dale: *How To Win Friends and Influence People,* 108
castle, 98-99
child(ren), 95
    divine, 70n, 73
    dreams of, 73-74
    collective, 92, 108
companionship, 76. *See also* relationship
compensation, 8, 15, 108, 115
complex(es), 23, 39-40, 43, 84-88, 100, 103. *See also* father complex; mother complex
conflict, 96-98, 120
conscious(ness), 32, 67, 72-73, 86-87, 96
creative/creativity, 37, 42-43, 71
    as complex, 43
    depression, 104
    and erotic feelings, 19
    living, 81
    mother of, 102
"Crystal Ball, The," 90-101

depression, 19, 94, 100, 102-104
    creative, 104
devouring mother, 92
Dingbat wine, 17, 19, 119
divine child, 70n, 73
doing vs. being, 32, 35, 40

Dolittle, Dr., 33
Don Juan, 51, 120
doo-doo, 32-33, 36-37, 118
doubling motif, 97. *See also* two
dream(s), 7, 15n, 41, 67, 101
  of ball(s), 7, 107-108, 119
  of ball games, 7, 21
  of breaking into house, 102
  of child(ren), 73-74
  of fecundating inner woman, 70n
  of hobbling on stumps, 41
  of Jung and lecture, 82-83
  of prison imagery, 48
  of puers and puellas, 48
  of Rachel, 43
  of receiving seed of inner man, 70n
  of spider on skis, 35
  of witch of the east, 41
Dummling, 55, 94-95, 100
dung. *See* beetle; doo-doo; shadow

eagle, 92-94
Edinger, E.F.: *The Sacred Psyche,* 73n
  Melville's Moby-Dick, 94
Eliot, T.S.: "The Love Song of J. Alfred
  Prufrock," 115-116
enchantress, 91-92. *See also* anima
enantiodromia, 50, 111, 115
energy gradient, 105-106
Eros/erotic, 19, 37-40, 42, 46, 49, 91

falling apart, 113-115
fantasies/fantasy, 33, 54
father complex, 39-40, 85, 112n
feet, 41
feminine, negative, 92, 94, 98, 98
Fields, Dorothy, 68
Fineglow, 109
forest, 100
Freud/Jung Letters, 29

gambling, 58-59
games, ball, 7, 11-12, 19, 20, 21, 24-27,
  37, 51. *See also* snooker

gargoyle, 77, 103
gaze/gazing, 85, 117
giant(s), 100
Gina, 61-65, 85
"Glass Mountain, The," 99
Goethe, Johann Wolfgang von, 28
golden balls, 26
good and better, bad and worse, 31-32
Great Mother, 102. *See also* mother complex
guilt, Promethean, 72

Haggard, H. Rider: *She,* 107n
Hannah, Barbara: *Jung: His Life and
  Work,* 29n
Harding, M. Esther: "The Meaning and
  Value of Depression," 103
  The Parental Image, 50n
hat, 100
Hephaestus, 28
Hefner, Hugh, 109
Hercules, 33, 98
hero/heroic, 28, 94-96
Hillman, James: "Betrayal," 114-115
hobbling, dream of, 41
Hollis, James: *On This Journey We Call
  Our Life,* 114
  Swamplands of the Soul, 75
Houdini, Harry, 38

imprisonment, 48
incest, 70
individuation, 19, 21, 24, 29, 31, 33, 37,
  51, 67, 80, 97, 113
inertia, 28
inferior function, 17, 95-96
infidelity, 29
inflation, 47
  negative, 68
infrared to ultraviolet, 22, 23
inner man/woman, dreams of, 70n
instinct(s), 22, 23, 31, 46, 49, 57, 78, 94-
  95, 98
  and archetype(s), 22, 23
  of truth, 51, 95

intermittent claudication, 82n
intimacy with distance, 113
intuition/intuitive(s), 17-18, 37, 78-79

Jackson, Eve: *Food and Transformation:*
  25n
Jessy Kate, 97n
Jung, C.G./Jungian, 16, 19, 25n, 52
  on abandonment, 67
  Aion, 65
  on alchemists, 75
  and Alcoholics Anonymous, 63n
  on analysis, 34
  on anima/animus, 40, 65, 99, 107n
  on archetype and instinct, 22, *23*
  on art, 42-43
  biographies of, 29n
  on Buridan's ass, 97-98
  on cap, 100
  on companionship, 76. *See also*
    relationship
  on complex(es), 87-88
  on conscious(ness), 67, 72-73
  "Definitions," 78
  on depression, 104
  "The Development of Personality," 31
  in dream, 82-83
  on energy, 105-106
  on Eros and Logos, 38-40
  The Freud/Jung Letters, 29
  on good and better, 31
  on hat, 100
  on instinct and archetype, 22-23
  "Instinct and the Unconscious," 23
  on libido, 106
  on loneliness, 72-76
  on love and power, 91
  and Marie-Louise von Franz, 60
  on marriage, 29
  Memories, Dreams, Reflections, 76
  model of typology, 17
  on mother complex, 93
  Mysterium Conunctionis, 38, 40
  "On the Nature of the Psyche," 22

"The Persona as a Segment of the
  Collective Psyche," 72
  on power and love, 91
  "Psychological Aspects of the Mother
    Archetype," 93
  "A Psychological Theory of Types," 87
  "The Psychology of the Child
    Archetype," 67, 70n, 73
  "The Psychology of the Transference,"
    34
  "Psychotherapists or the Clergy," 74
  "Psychotherapy and a Philosophy of
    Life," 88
  "On the Relation of Analytical
    Psychology to Poetry," 42
  "Religious Ideas in Alchemy," 75
  on the riddle of the Sphinx, 54n
  on sparks, 28
  "The Structure of the Unconscious," 98
  on suffering, 88
  "The Symbolic Life," 75
  Symbols of Transformation, 54n, 106
  and Toni Wolff, 29
  on transcendent function, 96n
  on transformation, 104
  Two Essays on Analytical Psychology,
    91, 105
Jung, Emma, 29n

Kafka, Franz, 68, 94
  The Castle, 98
Khepri, 32, 118
kairos, 111
Kern, Jerome, 68
knees, as seat of soul, 41
knife/knives, 24-25

lavender jelly, 34-35, 41
lecture, dream of, 82-83
libido, 104, 106
life/living, creative, 81
  like a ball/game, 19, 51
lingam, and yoni, 103n
lion, 92

liver, 93
Logos, 37-40, 91-92
loneliness, 67, 72-76, *See also* solitude
love, 61, 67, 76, 83, 91, 117
loverKnot(s), 118
loverNot(s), 52, 55, 81, 83, 113, 115-116
Luigi, 17, 92-97, 99, 101

mandala(s), 21
   exploded, 22
marriage, 112, 117
   and infidelity, 29
Mary Magdalene, 106
masculinity, 116
Matisse, Henri: *Les Joueurs de Boules,* 20
maya, 18
meditation, 32
Melville, Herman: *Moby-Dick,* 94
midlife, 16n, 116
mirror/mirroring, 17, 29, 53, 69, 80
moth, yucca, 23-24
mother, complex, 39, 57, 64, 83-85, 93-94,
   98, 108, 112n
   of creativity, 102
   devouring, 92
music of the spheres, 28, 119
mysterium coniunctionis, 99

narcissism, 8, 68
negative, feminine, 92, 94, 98
   inflation, 68
neurosis/neurotic, 48, 75, 88, 96, 104
night-sea journey, 100
numinous, 44n
Nurse Pam, 11, 16, 18, 24-25, 30-42, 44-
   52, 54-59, 78-99, 101-102, 112-118

O'Donohue, John: *Anam Cara,* 81n, 85n
Oedipus, 54
ol' blue eyes. *See* Sinatra, Frank
older women, 53
Onians, R.B. *The Origins of European
   Thought,* 41n
opposite(s), 49-50, 97, 105, 108

Pam. *See* Nurse Pam
Pam2, 33, 59, 114
paranoia, 102
Perera, Sylvia Brinton: *The Scapegoat
   Complex,* 87n
persona, 10, 35, 102
personality, 19, 21, 73, 86, 103-104
Peter Pan, 45
philosophical thinking, 22
Picture of Dorian Gray, The, 45
Plato: *Symposium,* 80n
power, 91
prima materia, 70
prison imagery, in dreams, 48
projection, 18-19, 45, 52, 66-67, 80, 114
Promethean guilt, 72
Prometheus, 93
psyche, self-regulation of the, 15, 67, 108
puer/puella, 45-49, 52, 93
Pythagoras, 28

Rachel, 33, 43, 68-76, 106-108, 119-120
regression, 102
relationship, 75, 80
riddle of the Sphinx, 54
Rolling Ball Theory, 28
Rolling Doo-Doo Theory, 32
Rolling Stones, 109

scapegoat(s), 87n
scarab beetle, 32, 118
schizophrenia, 100
"Sea Hare, The," 99
Self, 16n, 51, 100
self-regulation of the psyche, 15, 67, 108
senex, 8, 49, 51
sensation function, 17-18, 37, 53n, 78
shadow, 8, 17-18, 47, 49, 62, 70
Shakespeare, William: *All's Well That
   Ends Well,* 57, 94
"She who must be obeyed," 107
Simon & Garfunkle, 36
Sinatra, Frank, 20, 58, 68, 111
sleep. *See* big sleep

Sleeping Beauty, 69
snooker, 7, 26-27
solitude, 68, 70, 72, 74-76
Sons of Guns, 62
Sophia (Bible), 99
soror mystica, 70
soul, 22, 28, 88-89
  friend, 80-81. See also *anam cara*
  knees as seat of, 41
  loss of, 100
  mate, 80-81
spark(s)/sparkle, 18, 28, 52, 60, 66-67, 77,
  102, 105, 116
spectrum, 22, *23*
sphere(s), music of the, 28, 119
  soul as a, 22
Sphinx, 54
spider, as *maya,* 18
  on skis, dream of, 35
Stewart, Rod, 59, 117
stare/staring, 85n
Steinberg, Warren: *Circle of Care,* 104
Storr, Anthony: *Solitude,* 70-72, 103-104
Sunny, 30, 37
sweetheart(s), 80-81
symbol/symbolism, 7, 21, 32, 37, 41, 48,
  73, 90, 92-94, 98-100, 108

temenos, 47
tension, 52, 56, 70, 81, 105, 114
thinking symbolically, 90
toe(s), 34
touch/touching, 81n
transcendence, 8, 98
transcendent function, 96-97, 111
transformation, 32, 70, 72, 97, 100
  and depession, 104
transitional objects, 25
true bride, 113
truth, instinct of, 51, 95
turd, 8, 55, 70, 102, 119
twenty-three, 99

twenty-two, 99-100
two, 96-97
typology, Jung's model of, 17, 90

ultraviolet to infrared, 22-23
unconscious, 17, 19, 45, 88, 93, 95, 100
  as creative, 104
unexpected, the, 19
unfaithfulness, in marriage, 29

Von Franz, Marie-Louis, 41, 91n
  Alchemy: An Introduction, 51n
  Animus and Anima in Fairy Tales, 60
  C.G. Jung: His Myth in Our Time, 29n
  on hero, 95
  Interpretation of Fairy Tales, 91n, 95n
  and Jung, 60
  On Divination and Synchronicity, 97n
  Problem of the Puer Aeternus, 41n, 48n
  on puer psychology, 48
  on Self, 51

whale(s), 93-94
wholeness, 21, 70n. *See also* individuation
Wilhelm, Richard: *The I Ching,* 40n
will power, 8, 108
wind turbine, 89
wine, Dingbat, 17, 19, 119
Winnicott, D.W.: "Transitional Objects
  and Transitional Phenomena," 25n
wisdom, book of, 50, 120
Wisdom (Bible), 99
Wolff, Toni, 29, 37
Woodman, Marion, *The Pregnant Virgin,*
  40n
writing, 42

yang and yin, 40
Yeoman, Ann: *Now or Neverland,* 41n
yoni(s), 103
youthfulness, 45, 53
yucca moth, 23-24

Also by Daryl Sharp in this Series

Prices and Payment in $US (except in Canada, $Cdn)

THE SECRET RAVEN
Conflict and Transformation in the Life of Franz Kafka
ISBN 0-919123-00-7. (1980) 128 pp. $16

PERSONALITY TYPES: Jung's Model of Typology
ISBN 0-919123-30-9. (1987) 128 pp. Diagrams $16

THE SURVIVAL PAPERS: Anatomy of a Midlife Crisis
ISBN 0-919123-34-1. (1988) 160 pp. $18

DEAR GLADYS: The Survival Papers, Book 2
ISBN 0-919123-36-8. (1989) 144 pp. $18

JUNG LEXICON: A Primer of Terms and Concepts
ISBN 0-919123-48-1. (1991) 160 pp. Diagrams $18

GETTING TO KNOW YOU: The Inside Out of Relationship
ISBN 0-919123-56-2. (1992) 128 pp. $16

THE BRILLIG TRILOGY:

> **1. CHICKEN LITTLE: The Inside Story *(A Jungian Romance)***
> ISBN 0-919123-62-7. (1993) 128 pp. $16

> **2. WHO AM I, REALLY? Personality, Soul and Individuation**
> ISBN 0-919123-68-6. (1995) 144 pp. $18

> **3. LIVING JUNG: The Good and the Better**
> ISBN 0-919123-73-2. (1996) 128 pp. $16

JUNGIAN PSYCHOLOGY UNPLUGGED: My Life As an Elephant
ISBN 0-919123-81-3. (1998) 160 pp. $18

CUMULATIVE INDEX of Inner City Books: The First 80 Titles, 1980-1998
ISBN 0-919123-82-1. (1999) 160 pp. 8-1/2" x 11" $20

DIGESTING JUNG: Food for the Journey
ISBN 0-919123-96-1. (2001) 128 pp. $16

Discounts: any 3-5 books, 10%; 6-9 books, 20%; 10 or more, 25%
Add Postage/Handling: 1-2 books, $6 surface ($10 air); 3-4 books, $8 surface ($12 air);
  5-9 books, $15 surface ($20 air); 10 or more, $10 surface ($25 air)

Ask for **Jung at Heart** newsletter and complete Catalogue of **over 100 titles**

INNER CITY BOOKS
Box 1271, Station Q, Toronto, ON M4T 2P4, Canada

Tel. (416) 927-0355 / Fax (416) 924-1814 / E-mail: sales@innercitybooks.net